FELL'S GUIDE TO

BUYING OR BUILDING A HOME

FELL'S GUIDE TO BUYING, BUILDING AND FINANCING A HOME

by
M. ROBERT BEASLEY

FREDERICK FELL, INC., PUBLISHERS NEW YORK

Copyright © 1963 by Robert M. Beasley
All rights reserved. For information query:

    Frederick Fell, Inc.
    386 Park Ave. South
    New York 16, N. Y.

Printed in the United States of America

Library of Congress Catalog Card No. 63-21657

Published simultaneously in Canada by George McLeod, Ltd., Toronto, Ont.

Dreams Can Come True—With Advance Planning

Just as the steady dripping of single drops of water will eventually wear away solid rock, a consistent pattern of savings can attain seemingly insurmountable goals.

Substantial sums are not put aside overnight, or between a few paydays, but are acquired by a planned, systematic operation over a given period of time. Savings should be included in the family budget, with x number of dollars allocated each pay period for that specific purpose, placed on a "fixed expense" basis. Nothing should be allowed to interrupt that regular pattern. It is easy to develop the habit of "putting it off until next payday." Once this begins, the purpose of the savings is defeated, so, consider your savings as an obligation that must be met each month—and not as an arbitrary or voluntary thing. In reality it is a debt which you owe to yourself, to your family, to your future.

Realization of your dreams in life comes with advance planning. We all dream of sending Junior to college, of cruising around the world for our 20th anniversary, of any number of things we may some day achieve. Well, most dreams are possible—if money alone can make them materialize, but they don't come true by our sitting placidly back, relying on inherited money from a rich relative. That relative might use some of the money to maintain excellent health, and outlive you, so this has become a do-it-yourself world, in which one puts away savings as methodically as he nails misplaced shingles back onto his roof.

The accompanying chart shows the amounts that must be put aside each month, earning certain rates of interest, to provide the sums which you will need in the future. These figures are computed on deposits being made every month—not just

SAVINGS CHART

It will require regular monthly savings with interest rates listed below, compounded semi-annually, to attain your savings goal.

Amount to be Saved	No. of years money will be needed	2-1/2%	3%	3-1/2%	4%	5%	6%
$ 500	5 years	$ 7.85	$ 7.80	$ 7.70	$ 7.60	$ 7.45	$ 7.25
	10 years	3.70	3.60	3.50	3.40	3.25	3.10
	15 years	2.35	2.20	2.15	2.05	1.90	1.50
	20 years	1.60	1.55	1.45	1.40	1.25	1.10
$1,000	5 years	$15.75	$15.55	$15.40	$15.25	$14.85	$14.55
	10 years	7.40	7.25	7.05	6.90	6.50	6.20
	15 years	4.65	4.45	4.25	4.10	3.80	3.50
	20 years	3.25	3.10	2.90	2.75	2.45	2.20
$2,000	5 years	$31.50	$31.15	$30.80	$30.45	$29.75	$29.05
	10 years	14.75	14.40	14.05	13.70	13.05	12.40
	15 years	9.20	8.85	8.55	8.20	7.60	7.00
	20 years	6.45	6.15	5.80	5.50	4.95	4.40

Dreams Can Come True—With Advance Planning

$3,000	5 years 10 years 15 years 20 years	$47.25 22.15 13.85 9.70	$46.70 21.60 13.30 9.20	$46.15 21.10 12.80 8.75	$45.65 20.55 12.30 8.30	$44.60 19.55 11.40 7.40	$43.60 18.60 10.50 6.65
$4,000	5 years 10 years 15 years 20 years	$63.00 29.50 18.45 12.95	$62.30 28.80 17.75 12.30	$61.55 28.10 17.10 11.65	$60.90 27.40 16.40 11.05	$59.50 26.10 15.20 9.90	$58.10 24.80 14.00 8.85
$5,000	5 years 10 years 15 years 20 years	$78.75 36.90 23.05 16.20	$77.85 36.00 22.20 15.35	$76.95 35.25 21.35 14.55	$76.10 34.25 20.55 13.80	$74.35 32.60 19.00 12.35	$72.65 31.00 17.50 11.05
$6,000	5 years 10 years 15 years 20 years	$94.50 44.30 27.65 19.40	$93.40 43.20 26.60 18.40	$92.35 42.20 25.60 17.45	$91.30 41.10 24.65 16.55	$89.20 39.10 22.75 14.85	$87.20 37.20 21.00 13.25

occasionally, when there is nothing else you care to do with the money. While multiples in the chart only extend to $6,000, higher amounts can be computed simply, by moving the decimal point. For instance, if you wish to save $10,000 at 4 per cent over a 20-year period, it would require $27.50 per month, that is, the amount listed under $1,000 at 4 per cent for 20 years ($2.75) with the decimal point moved over one place.

Take a few minutes now, to evaluate your hopes, dreams and plans into dollars and years, and determine what steps you can take, at this time, to make your years ahead more complete and happy. You'll probably be surprised at how small that "insurmountable barrier" becomes when it is broken down into monthly installments.

M. Robert Beasley

TABLE OF CONTENTS

INTRODUCTION: DREAMS CAN COME TRUE—
WITH ADVANCE PLANNING v

Chapter   Page

1 YOUR SELECTION OF—AND DEALINGS WITH—
   REAL ESTATE PEOPLE.................   1
   The Language of Real Estate   5

2 THINGS TO KNOW BEFORE BUILDING A HOME.   12
   Securing Plans and Specifications   13
   1. An Architect   14
   2. Plan Service Agencies   14
   Selecting the Contractor   14
   Completion Bond   15
   Necessary Building Insurance   16
   Special Assessments   17
   General Contract Conditions   18
   Financial Arrangements: Owner-Contractor   21
   Owner-Contractor Relationship   22
   The Closing   23

3 SELECTING YOUR BUILDING LOT   25
   Neighborhood   25
   Grading   26
   Lot Shape   28

	Soil Check	28
	Landscaping	29
	Your Water Supply	29
	Municipal Facilities	29
	Property Lines	30
	Zoning Laws and Building Codes	31
	Taxes and Assessments	32
	Easements and Rights-of-Way	33
	Condemnation	34
	Professional Assistance	34
4	PROPERLY ORIENT YOUR HOME	36
	Proper Home Orientation	37
	Heating	38
	Cooling	38
	Breezes	39
	Natural Light	40
	House and Garden as a Unit	40
	Trees	41
	Patio and Terrace	41
	Plumbing and Water	41
	Closing	42
5	HOW TO BUY AN EXISTING HOME	43
	General Conditions	44
	Foundation	45
	Basement	46
	Roof	47
	Attic	48

Contents

	Insulation	49
	Heating	51
	Plumbing	52
	Electrical	53
	Paint	54
	Termites	55
	Room Arrangement	56
	Kitchen and Bath	57
6	DISPOSING OF YOUR OLD HOME	59
	Trade Your Present Home	59
	Selling Your Old House	61
	Selling by Yourself	65
	Proper Advertising	65
	Repairs Prior to Sale	66
	Keep Your House Furnished	67
	Answering Questions	68
	Don't Use a Hard Sell	68
	Follow Up Prospects	69
	Price Flexibility	69
	Legal Assistance	69
7	WHAT YOU SHOULD KNOW ABOUT FINANCING AND MORTGAGES	71
	Shopping for the Mortgage	72
	Questions the Lending Institution Will Ask You	73
	Length of Mortgage	73
	Types of Mortgages	76
	Conventional Mortgage	76

	VA Guaranteed Mortgages	77
	FHA-Insured Mortgage	77
	Construction Loans	78
	Hidden Costs	78
8	TRICKS IN SAVING MONEY WHEN BUILDING ..	83
	Architect	85
	General Contractor	85
	Sub-Contracting	87
	Materials	90
	Electrical	91
	Plumbing	93
	Heating	93
	Air Conditioning	94
	Other Construction	95
	Lawns	95
	Protect Your Material—Fair Warning	96
	Building Cost Breakdown Chart	98
	Chart of Free Services Available to Home Builders From Electric Power Companies ...	99
9	WHAT TO DO BEFORE—DURING—AND AFTER MOVING.............................	110
	Moving Insurance.......................	111
	Before You Move	113
	Utilities.............................	115
	Financial Responsibilities	116
	Household Duties	116
	Family Obligations......................	117

Contents

    After the Move 118
    If You Do Your Own Packing... 119
    Doing Your Own Moving 121

10 LEARNING TO LIVE WITH YOUR NEW HOME 122
    Builder's Responsibility 123
    The Terrible Trio 124
    Shrinkage 125
    Swelling 125
    General Builder Liability 126
    Foundation Cracks 127
    Ceilings and Walls 127
    Interior Concrete Floors................. 127
    Roof 128
    Floors 128
    Walls................................. 128
    Warping Doors 129
    Wet Basement 129
    Heating System 129
    Appliances 130

11 A GUIDE TO DECORATING YOUR NEW HOME—
    ALL ABOUT COLOR 131

FELL'S GUIDE TO

BUYING OR BUILDING A HOME

Chapter I

YOUR SELECTION OF — AND DEALINGS WITH — REAL ESTATE PEOPLE

Whether you buy an existing home, or sell your old one, you'll probably require the services of a qualified real estate agent. There are more than a half million real estate salesmen in the United States, and the success of your buying or selling will depend a great deal upon your wisdom in making this choice. Whether you are buying or selling, you have a large investment at stake; so, protect that investment by taking a few hours to investigate the agent you choose to represent you.

Your real estate agent becomes an important part of your life at the time you decide to buy or sell. He is your official representative, your "middle man," charged with the responsibility of bringing you together with persons who either wish to buy your home, or to sell you another one. The agent assists in negotiating contracts, making appointments, and, generally, he protects your interests. For this, he is entitled to a rate of commission which is determined by law and based on percentage —usually 5 per cent of the total house price, or 10 per cent for the negotiations of unimproved land.

In a sense, anyone arranging for the sale or lease of someone else's property, assumes the role of "agent." The term "broker," is generally confined to the proprietors or principal members of a real estate firm. The salesmen who work for brokers are usually called "agents." There is also a big difference between a "Realtor" and a "Real Estate Agent." Only real estate people who are members of the National Association of Real Estate Boards, or its affiliated local boards, can use the trademark and designation of "Realtor." The association has strict rules and regulations, and a code of ethics, to insure and maintain competence and good conduct within the real estate business. All members are pledged to ethical standards, and must abide by them. Because of the rigid standards under which they operate, you can be reasonably sure of fair dealings with anyone qualified to call himself a Realtor.

The designation of Realtor, for instance, prohibits a broker from representing both buyer and seller in any one transaction —a system in which, when resorted to by unethical real estate people, everyone but the agent gets hurt. Such a designation would also prohibit a broker from engaging in the sale of any property in which he has a personal financial interest—another bad practice sometimes used by unscruptulous real estate men. There are many controls, imposed upon authorized realtors, that do not restrict the ordinary real estate salesman or agent. Since you will be investing a considerable sum of your money, this free, added margin of protection should be enjoyed, for Realtors charge the same basic fees as do others in the field, who are not responsible to a national board, and do not risk revocation of their licenses.

Another pitfall that many home buyers and sellers fall into, is the selection of part-time agents. Unfortunately, there are persons throughout the country, with local and state license for real estate activity, who put only a few hours a day—or even a week—into the business. This is a favorite field for retired persons, housewives, young men seeking some part-time income, and for the rank amateur—lured into the field by stories of big earnings. Choosing an inefficient or dilatory representative can be costly, both in money and in time, and can create disappointments and headaches. So, again, it is best to select a well-established Realtor who knows his business.

It is best to make your selection from those Realtors who specialize in handling private homes, for many, devoting most of their time to commercial property, may be out of touch with the individual home market. A good broker will not agree to sell your house until after he had made a thorough inspection of the property—attic to basement, inside and out. He will ask the seller numerous questions, in order to receive answers which will enable him intelligently to answer the pertinent questions of prospective buyers (so don't think he is nosey or inquisitive, but answer his questions honestly and fairly).

Your Selection of-and Dealings with-Real Estate People

In selling through a Realtor, you take advantage of his years of experience in the local markets, and of his perpetual list of prospective buyers who might be interested in your property. He also works with numerous other Realtors with whom your property will be listed, and this, in effect, means that you'll have many competent real estate men working toward the sale of your property, at the cost of just one commission. He will get together with you on a fair market value, set the asking price, advise you whether or not to put a "mark-up" into the price to give him leeway for bargaining, and he will suggest ways of making the property more attractive to prospective buyers. He also knows the best media in which to advertise your particular property, and will guard your interests throughout the sale. Most Realtors work closely with reputable attorneys, but this does not mean that you should go through any property settlement without formal legal advice.

If you are buying, you will not commission the Realtor or agent, but when you have checked his business reputation—and found it above reproach—you can usually put your faith in him. Although the seller will be paying him commission, he will still make every effort to satisfy your desires, and will make his entire listing—as well as the listings of other Realtors—available for your inspection and selection. His years of experience are, again, at your disposal regarding fairness in price, good property construction, proper financing, and general negotiations.

Check with your friends and neighbors as to the Realtor who handled their buying and selling. Everyone has a definite opinion of the fairness, ability and enterprise shown by the real estate people who have previously handled their transactions, so, listen to their recommendations and complaints, and decide for yourself as to the one who will be the most logical choice for your needs. Check, also, with at least two or three banks or building and loan associations. They will be glad to recommend Realtors who have dealt with them over the years, and a recommendation from this source is usually important, as these institutions will detect and denounce even the slightest unethical activities. Then, having made a tentative selection, visit the Realtor's office to get an idea as to the property he handles, and of the efficiency of his operation.

Be emphatic about having a clear understanding of the commission to be charged you. Many areas have a recommended scale of commissions, but others leave this to individual transactions, where a figure is worked out between client and Realtor; so, don't wait for the sale to be consummated, and then be annoyed and surprised by the amount of commission charged. If possible, get your man's figures, and time element, into writing.

In short, when listing your home for sale, have the Realtor put into writing the agreed sales price, the minimum terms acceptable by you, the time element and nature of his listings, and the commission upon which you two have agreed.

Sometimes, when a house has been widely advertised, it becomes difficult to ascertain whether the ultimate buyer was procured through the Realtor's services or just through happenchance luck. When this situation develops, frequent disputes arise between broker and seller as to wheter a commission has been earned. Be fair in such a case. The advertising has caused much word-of-mouth publicity, so concede any points that might be doubtful. When such disputes go to court for settlement, the broker usually wins, and you will only have to pay additional court costs.

Legally, most brokers have merely to produce a ready, willing and able prospect to buy a particular property at the seller's asking price, at the seller's terms, and he has earned his commission. Once he has fulfilled this obligation, if you decide to not sell to that person, the broker can force payment of his commission, and, while you have the prerogative of changing your mind and not selling, you would still be responsible for payment of the commission—so be sure you definitely want to sell before engaging a Realtor's services.

There is also another point to keep in mind when buying through a Real Estate agent. Statements made by him, in showing the property, are generally neither official nor enforceable. Glib answers may be supplied by unscrupulous agents about zoning, restrictions, taxes, assessments, easements, rights-of-way and future development plans for the neighborhood, but they should not be accepted simply because he tells you such situations exist. In most cases, agents will answer such questions honestly, but it is best to double check the

Your Selection of- and Dealings with- Real Estate People   5

answers through appropriate municipal agencies. A trip to City Hall will often give all the answers a prospective property buyer needs.

THE LANGUAGE OF REAL ESTATE

During the process of buying or selling a home, you will be subjected to many confusing, esoteric words and phrases, which will, in many cases, be actually misleading—unless you are familiar with their exact meaning and intent. For the uninitiated, real estate transactions, in themselves, are sufficiently complex without the buyer or seller's being unable to fully comprehend what the vitally important conversations and contract clauses truly mean. For this reason, you will do well to familiarize yourself with the terms and phrases most likely to be met with in a property transaction.

ABSTRACT: This is oten referred to as the "Abstract of Title." In effect, it is a legal survey of the property, back to the beginning of property records which establishes clear, uncontested ownership, up to and including the date of survey.

AMORTIZATION: This implies dissolving a loan, or, more specifically, a mortgage, by means of a process of regular payments. Under normal conditions the period of amortization is the number of years the mortgage is designated to run. Where future plans include paying off the mortgage before the specified number of years, an "amortization clause" should be included in the contract, so that the mortgage can be liquidated before the given number of years, without heavy penalties.

APPRAISAL: Evaluation of a given property by a professional real estate man, to determine true value. The lending institution will usually require an appraisal before advancing money. Such appraisals are generally conservative, computed more upon market value, or the amount that could be obtained in a quick foreclosure sale, than on the actual price. Cost of such appraisal is paid by the person buying the property, with the report being submitted to the lending institution. Where specific request is made for a copy of the appraisal, copies will be supplied to the buyer.

BROKERAGE: Brokerage systems are the backbone of the real estate business. Brokers, for a fee or commission, assist persons in buying or selling homes or unimproved property. Through this system a home can be listed with numerous agencies, with the seller paying only one commission.

CERTIFICATE OF OCCUPANCY: This is one of the papers you should insist upon receiving at time of settlement. It should specifically certify that the home has been examined by local health and building departments, and that the premises are healthy and safe for occupancy. This should be accompanied by other certificates to the effect that plumbing, electrical, and sanitary facilities, adequately installed, will meet with municipal codes and requirements.

CERTIFICATE OF TITLE: See: Deed

CLOSING COSTS: Frequently referred to as "Settlement Costs," these include all miscellaneous expenses pertinent to purchasing a home. At such a time you will be expected to pay any charges involved in mortage services, title insurance and search, recording stamps for the deed, fees for appraisal, survey charges, federal and local taxes, credit reports, advance tax, insurance, and water estimates—and any other charges peculiar to your institution or area. Many times these charges can be included in the total mortgage; in other cases they must be paid for in cash, over and above the basic amount of mortgage. Determine from your attorney or Realtor how much cash you may need for this final phase.

COLLATERAL: Sometimes a cash pledge is required to guarantee oral or written agreements. This sum, as a rule comparatively small, is called collateral. A builder is often called upon for collateral to guarantee a specific performance of the work that will be done. A buyer is sometimes asked for collateral to guarantee against loss for taking the property off the active market.

COMPLETION BOND: A much overlooked document in building a home, this is a bond posted by the builder guaranteeing that a specific home will be completed at a given time, and it also insures against loss should the builder become financially unable to complete the building. This guarantee is underwritten by insurance companies who check into the builder's reputation and past performance record, denying such bonds where builders have not been faithful or competent in previous dealings. They are issued to reliable builders, at nominal cost, so, should a builder seem reluctant to post such a bond, you may assume there is some reason for such reluctance, and that his reputation and background should be thoroughly investigated before you proceed any further.

COMPREHENSIVE INSURANCE: An addition to regular insurance policies that provides coverage against windstorm, falling aircraft, acts of God, and similar possibilities. Premiums are usually very low for this added coverage, and they are well worth the small extra amount of money.

CONVENTIONAL MORTGAGE: This implies any non-government mortgage loan, where the money has been provided by an individual, a bank, savings and loan association, or similar lending institution. The conventional mortgage generally has the higher interest rate—plus such attractive features as being readily accessible and much quicker to negotiate; it also involves less complicated procedures. Such mortgages usually require at least a 20 per cent down payment, and they rarely exceed 20 years in duration.

DEED: This is frequently called the "Certificate of Title," and is the official legal document establishing ownership of any property or building.

DEED OF TRUST: A few states use this vehicle in place of a mortgage, but it is essentially the same as a mortgage. The difference is that a third party, usually an established institution, retains the security in trust for the lender, rather than the lender holding the deed, as in cases of mortgages.

DEPRECIATION: The natural process of a house reducing in value through normal, everyday, wear and tear. Normally this is computed each year at the rate of from 2 to 3 per cent of the total value.

EARNEST MONEY: This is a sum the prospective buyer advances to establish good faith in offering to buy a certain piece of property, and it is frequently referred to as "Hand Money." This nominal sum is generally posted at the time the "offer to purchase" is signed, and is applied to the down payment when the seller accepts the offer. In cases where the prospective buyer decides not to complete the transaction, such money becomes the legal property of the seller. Where the buyer might not be able to secure adequate mortgage, or should the house not meet specifications as presented, the buyer can refuse to consummate the purchase and the money is returned to him. All particulars and specifications should be put into writing when this time advance money is posted.

EASEMENT: An absolute right granted for use of the property, although such property does not belong to the organization involved. Usually limited in scope, this right is consigned to utility companies, roads, etc. Easements run with the land and usually cannot be cancelled by present owners. They are generally for installation of pipe, sewage, utility lines, etc., under, over or through properties, for general community benefit. Previous agreements of this sort are always written into land records and such conditions can quickly and easily be determined before purchase of a property.

EQUITY: This indicates the amount of the particular home or property you own. As mortgage payments are made, your equity in the property increases.

ESCROW: Securities, money, etc., held by a third party, usually a bank or mortgage company, until certain specified conditions are fully met. This places the money out of control of both parties involved in the transaction, since the third party only pays such funds when terms of that particular contract are fulfilled. A good example of this is at

Your Selection of- and Dealings with- Real Estate People

closing, or settlement time, where some features of the house might not meet all agreed terms. The lending institution will withhold a sufficient amount of money from the full price to guarantee that these conditions are fulfilled, and will pay out the money withheld only at the time and circumstances agreed to by you and the builder. There is usually a time limit on escrow money, to avoid unnecessary delay in accomplishing the required task.

EXCLUSIVE AGENCY: With this form of contract, only the broker who has the listing can be your agent. If you sell the property yourself, you do not have to pay a commission. If you sell the property to anyone produced by a broker who is not directly associated with your broker, you owe your broker a commission to the broker producing the buyer.

EXCLUSIVE RIGHT TO SELL: This is the most restrictive form of contract between seller and broker. With this arrangement, the broker is entitled to his commission, even if you should sell the property yourself. This type of program is used when the seller wants the broker to make an "all out" effort for a quick sale. Since he must make the sale to collect the commission, he usually gives exceptional service. Be sure to put a time limit on such an agreement.

F.H.A. MORTGAGE: Anyone who meets the basic requirements can obtain an FHA mortgage. The particular property, however, must pass the FHA minimum property standards; this is a built-in protection for the buyer. The government has a representative inspect the property for sound construction and to make sure there are no major shortcomings or defects. Down payments are 3 per cent on the first $15,000, 10 per cent from $15,000 to $20,000, and 25 per cent over $20,000—with low interest rates, and up to 35 years allowed for repayment. Because it is a government-insured loan, it passes through several different U.S. departments, and takes longer to obtain than the conventional mortgage.

FIRST PAPERS: Quite frequently called the "Offer to Purchase," these papers are completed by the prospective buyer, and when they are signed by both seller and prospective buyer they become binding on both parties. This document of good faith frequently leads to trouble unless all terms are very clearly and fully put into writing. As an alternate, have your attorney draw up a formal contract, where everything can be clearly set forth concerning both parties.

HAND MONEY: See: Earnest Money

LISTING: When you engage a broker to sell your property, he will "list" it among the other properties he has for sale. To avoid misunderstandings, the "listing" agreement between broker and seller should be in writing, setting forth every factor and stipulation.

MORTGAGE REDEMPTION INSURANCE: This is a combination of ordinary life and term insurance that will, for approximately one per cent of the mortgage value, provide life insurance on your unpaid mortgage. Should you die before the mortgage is paid, your family receives a clear title to the property. If you outlive the mortgage, there is usually sufficient cash surrender value accumulated on the ordinary life part of the policy to liquidate the mortgage a few years early.

MORTGAGEE: This term refers to the person or institution that lends the money, holding the property as security for the investment amount.

MORTGAGOR: This term refers to the person who borrows the money from the lending institution, or to the buyer.

MULTIPLE LISTING: This is a special arrangement among a group of brokers, whereby any property listed with any one of them, automatically receives listing with all of them. Only one commission is paid, since the brokers work on a reciprocal or split-fee basis. As with all other broker contracts, a time limit should be established in this type of arrangement.

OFFER TO PURCHASE: See: First Papers

OPEN END MORTGAGE: Under this type of arrangement, additional money can be borrowed on the original loan, through forthcoming years, for improvements, maintenance, appliances, etc., without creating a new mortgage and its fundamental costs. Payments may be increased to meet the new loan, or the mortgage may be extended to cover the addition.

OPEN LISTING: With this type arrangement you can list property for sale with as many brokers as you wish. A commission is due to only the broker who produces the prospect who actually buys the house.

RIDER: This is an addition to an insurance policy, mortgage, or contract, that adds new protection, clauses, or stipulations to the original agreement.

RIGHT OF WAY: Similar to Easements, whereby the city, county, previous owners, or utility companies have secured a guarantee to use certain portions of the property, even though they do not own such property.

SETTLEMENT See: Closing.

SURVEY: An actual survey to determine the exact property lines of a given piece of property. This is a very important step unless property lines are clearly defined and verified. The buyer usually pays for this service.

TAX ASSESSMENT: This is over and above regular taxes, usually imposed for special improvements, such as new sewage, paved streets, etc. All property owners benefitting from such improvements are assessed an equal proportion of the cost, according to property value. This potential of forthcoming assessments should be checked carefully before buying a new home.

TITLE INSURANCE: This inexpensive insurance is for the protection of property owners and mortgage holders, in order that no prioer claims will be filed against the property, and to guarantee that no legal flaws are contained in the title. Make it a point that both you—and the lending institution—be covered on this phase, as frequently, only the lending agency receives coverage up to the amount of their loan.

VA MORTGAGE: Under provisions of this type, mortgage, available to veterans of World War II who must apply before January 25, 1967, and Korean War Veterans, who must apply before January 31, 1975, property can most often be bought with no down payment, and at the very lowest interest rates. A nonveteran can assume such an advantageous mortgage where he buys the property from a veteran and just takes over the existing mortgage.

WAIVER OF LIENS: The builder should be made to supply a waiver of liens at the time of settlement, before he receives full payment. This certifies that he has paid all costs of materials, sub contractors, appliance installation, and all other costs involved in building your home, and absolves the home owner from future claims that might be placed against him.

ZONING: Zoning laws pertaining to the area in which your new home will be located should be checked carefully. While they might appear to be restricting, they actually protect your investment by guaranteeing that the neighborhood will not deteriorate within the near future. They might also interfere with your furture plans, such as not allowing swimming pools, offices in the home, a limit on TV antennas, etc., so check on both factors before signing a final agreement to purchase any home. Full records of zoning laws are available to the public at city and twon halls at no cost.

Chapter II

THINGS TO KNOW BEFORE BUILDING A HOME

Next to your marriage, building a home will probably be the biggest contract you will enter into during your lifetime. It will probably involve more money than you will spend on any other one thing, but it will provide more comfort, enjoyment and pride than any other material possession you acquire.

Building a home can either be a once in a lifetime pleasure, or the biggest nightmare you ever experienced. The difference between the two extremes hinges on a little advance knowledge of the pattern and intricacies of contracts and relationship with the contractor.

As with marriage, you must know specifically what you desire before entering into a contract. In marriage, this is a matter of finding the right mate. In building, satisfaction is achieved by securing specifications and plans that outline precisely what you wish in your home; how you wish it built; how much it is going to cost.

In marriage, once you find the right mate, you make arrangements with the preacher, to make your dreams come true. In building, once you secure specific plans and specifications, you make arrangements with a contractor to put your dreams into reality. Unlike marriage, which is worked out on an individual basis, frequently charting the course underway, building a home involves a definite pattern. By following the prescribed course set in this book, you can build a home, an addition to your existing building, or an entire housing development—without fear or nightmare complications.

IMPORTANCE OF SPECIFICATIONS

The contractor can be held legally responsible for only the materials and construction of the house as described in the specifications and drawings.

Since these are his absolute guides, extra caution should be exerted to guarantee that the drawings and specifications submitted cover every feature desired. Items forgotten, or purposely omitted, during listing automatically become "extras" and they must be paid for over and above the contracted price.

In addition to materials, proper specifications include work to be done through listing the necessary individual building operations under general classifications; excavating and grading; concrete work; masonry; carpentry; roofing and sheet metal; plumbing; heating; painting, etc. Under concrete work, for example, would be included such necessary items as footings, foundations, basement floor, walks, etc., each with thickness, depth, and grade material. Each and every phase of the building is covered in this manner in the specifications.

There are some common practises in different trades which frequently promote misunderstandings, unless definite terms are laid out from the beginning. For instance, the electrical work includes installations, such as outlets, and, when specified, kitchen fans, connections to furnace and range, doorbells, etc. Many times the lighting fixtures are purchased separately by the owner, architect or contractor—with the owner paying for installation. In other cases, a "lump sum" is stipulated to provide for electrical fixtures. Hardware specifications generally include only rough hardware, such as garage and sliding door hardware, nails, bolts, screws, etc. Finished hardware— door knobs, locks, hinges, and other metal trim—is usually selected and paid for by the owner or architect during construction. Go over each of these phases with the contractor, to insure your having a complete home, even after the building is finished.

SECURING PLANS AND SPECIFICATIONS

Good plans and specifications are the first, most important necessities in building a home. Before you enter into negotiations for plans and specifications, a family council should be held to develop an intelligent list of your combined needs, number of rooms, size, type and other personal desires. Once you decide exactly what you want, it then becomes a question of fitting your needs to available money. If, like most families, you have financial limitations, make your needs and desires flexible, to allow for variations, substitutions and other changes that may ultimately be required from the financial standpoint.

There are several ways to secure plans and specifications:

1. <u>An Architect.</u>

By hiring a registered architect, you are assured that drawings and specifications will be accurate and complete, with the house planned and designed to your individual needs and desires. His fee for plans and building supervision, which can be included and financed in the over all cost of the house, runs from 6 to 15 per cent of the total house cost. An architect who merely supplies the plans and specifications, but does not supervise the actual building, charges a fee ranging from 5 to 8 per cent of the total cost of the home.

2. <u>Plan Service Agencies.</u>

House plans and specifications, prepared by registered architects, are available through home building magazines and from material dealers. Costs of such plans run from $10 to $35, for the required set of four. These "package plans" are competently constructed, and sufficient for building. One disadvantage in securing plans from this source, is that revisions or changes are relatively limited. Whatever changes or revisions you desire must be competently written and recorded, before they can be used intelligently by your builder. Generally, a wide-enough range of these "stock" plans and specifications is available, to offer just about everything desired in a modern home. The savings, between the cost of such plans and an architect's fee, usually makes it a paying proposition to do without a few "little things" that you would normally include in your new home.

SELECTING THE CONTRACTOR

When an architect is employed, the usual method of selecting a contractor is through competitive bidding by equally competent, responsible contractors. The architect issues plans and specifications to each contractor with instructions covering the basis upon which the bid is to be let. Usually the contractor who meets all qualifications, and who has the lowest bid, is the one selected. Where no one of them submits a bid sufficiently low to conform to your desired investment, deletions and substitutions may be worked out, and new revised plans submitted, until a satisfactory bid is received. Any such changes are automatically made in the plans and specifications.

Where a contractor is selected by the individual owner, recommendations should be secured from lending agencies, building supply dealers, inspectors, or friends who have recently had work done by contractors. Since the builder will be in complete charge of all money designated for your home, he should be carefully chosen. You should ascertain that he has a good financial rating; that his reputation and integrity are good; that he has proven his ability to complete jobs satisfactorily, on schedule; that he has the experience, intelligence and compatible trade relations to provide you with the best in material and workmanship. Secure names of recent clients from the contractor you think best qualified, and talk to such people. They will be quick to give you his bad points as well as the good ones experienced during their dealings. Look at some of the houses the contractor has built over the years, for they will give you insight to his ability. Select a contractor who specializes in residential homes, since he will be better informed about housing developments of the latest designs than would a contractor who might specialize in supermarkets or filling stations.

Make price your secondary objective. The reputation and qualification of the contractor are more important than the few hundred dollars you might shave off the total cost. By "shopping around" for price, you are more vulnerable to falling prey to an unqualified, or a fly-by-night builder who might prove disastrous to your building budget and plans.

COMPLETION BOND

Having the contractor post a completion bond can be your best form of protection while building a home. Primarily, the ability of the contractor to post such a bond indicates that the bonding company has sufficient confidence in his work and integrity to provide this insurance. Bonding companies check into the past performances of the contractor, determining his reliability and capabilities, before issuing such a bond. If the contractor has previously pulled shady deals, missed completion dates, or caused clients to lose money, bonding companies will not cover his contract with a completion bond. When a contractor is unable to produce such a bond, the situation should be viewed suspiciously, with thought given to the selection of a builder of more stable reputation who can post a completion bond.

The completion bond also insures you against loss should the contractor become physically or financially unable to complete your home. Under such conditions the bonding company would assume the responsibility of having another contractor finish the job, without additional cost to you. This type of bond is not expensive, and it would be a smart investment to pay these premiums yourself if the contractor objects because of the added cost factor. Few reputable contractors or builders will object to posting a completion bond. If the contractor you choose manifests this reluctance, a further check into his background is definitely indicated.

NECESSARY BUILDING INSURANCE

WORKMEN'S COMPENSATION INSURANCE is a must for any construction work. Courts have consistently ruled that injured employees of uninsured contractors may claim damages from the homeowner. Insist that your contractor provide a certificate of adequate compensation insurance coverage. Any contractor who does not carry such insurance should be considered as not being financially responsible. Serious thought should be given before trusting him with your money, and with the building of your home. Without this vital protection, a workman who falls from a ladder, is struck by a falling board, or is hurt in any manner, could cost you the entire price of your home, plus your savings.

PUBLIC LIABILITY INSURANCE, also of great importance, is the contractor's responsibility. This type of coverage guarantees that you will not be held responsible for personal injury or property damage incurred during the building process. Check with your attorney and insurance agent about the advisability of providing your own "attractive nuisance" coverage. This provides direct coverage for children who might be hurt while playing around the job, etc.

FIRE AND THEFT INSURANCE should be carried by the contractor under a lump-sum contract; otherwise, the owner must assume this responsibility. Thousands of dollars in material will be evident at the building site, and many thieves specialize in pilfering from private construction locations. This kind of insurance, relatively inexpensive, can be worked out on a short term basis to cover only the period of time during building, until you assume occupancy of the home. While you are discussing this with your agent, inquire about extended coverage to include such vandalism as children breaking picture windows, tearing out fixtures, etc. This protection can be incorporated into your policy for just a few extra dollars.

TITLE INSURANCE is usually required by the lending institution. This is a relatively low, one premium type coverage that relieves you of responsibility in case of a defect in the land title. Should there be a prior lien against the property, unpaid taxes, claims by missing heirs, etc. the insurance company assumes responsibility and costs. Even when buying a development house, you simultaneously purchase the ground under and around the building at the same time, therefore a title search, and title insurance, are definitely necessary. Make your desire for title insurance known to your attorney at the start of negotiations. Where the lending institution is securing its own title search and insurance, you can include your protection at the same time, thus deriving savings on the premium.

SPECIAL ASSESSMENTS

While your attorney is arranging for title search and insurance, have him thoroughly investigate such special assessments as you are likely to encounter in the immediate future. Where streets and curbs are not already available for service to your new home, the builder should be responsible to the municipality for providing them. Have this factor included in your contract to avoid later misunderstanding and, possibly, unexpected expense. If the contractor does not assume this responsibility, check with the municipal authorities as to their installing such facilities, and whether or not you will be assessed for the installations. Storm sewers, sanitary plumbing, and other public utilities should be available to your property. If they aren't, check again with municipal authorities, or with the utility companies, about such installations, and learn where costs will be levied against you.

If you are going to be burdened with several different assessments within the immediate future, these expenditures must be added to the total cost of your new home. The additional figures might make the difference in whether or not you can afford the home. It is essential to have such matters clearly understood, and in writing, before investing your money—and while you can still change your mind. To suddenly find yourself deeply obligated afterward, when you can't do a thing about the indebtedness, might make all the difference in your ability to meet payments.

GENERAL CONTRACT CONDITIONS

Subject	Contractor Liability	Owner Liability
INSURANCE AND COMPENSATION	Contractor pays and maintains workmen's compensation, public liability, private liability and property damage insurance. He is responsible for damages or injury due to his acts or negligence, and to the actions of his workers.	Pays and maintains fire, and extended coverage, insurance during construction. Materials, forms, scaffolding and supplies should be covered, but not tools.
	In lump-sum contracts, the contractor owns material and theft insurance is his responsibility.	In cost-plus arrangements, owner pays for theft insurance, personal coverage of liability, in addition

Things to Know Before Building a Home

Subject	Contractor Liability	Owner Liability
INSURANCE AND COMPENSATION (Cont'd.)	In lump-sum contracts, the contractor owns material and theft insurance is his responsibility.	In cost-plus arrangements, owner pays for theft insurance, personal coverage of liability, in addition to contractor's.
BUILDING CODES AND ORDINANCES	Contractor is responsible for observing local, state and federal ordinances, and other laws covering work, supplying protection to owner from any damages for violations.	
PERMITS	Depending on locale, contractor often secures permits, building, utility, gas, electricity, water, etc.	Some localities require owner to obtain building permits. Some utility companies hold securing of utility permits is the owner's responsibility.
TAXES	Contractor pays social security on employees. In lump-sum contract he absorbs all material taxes, sales tax, etc.	Property tax is paid by owner. In cost-plus arrangement, owner also absorbs all taxes on materials.
SURVEY	No responsibility.	Owner pays for survey of property.

Subject	Contractor Liability	Owner Liability
ADDITIONAL CONTRACTOR EXPENSES	During construction, contractor pays labor, water, power, equipment, royalties, licenses, and other expenses protecting his work from damage. Defends all claims of infringement on patents. Maintains sanitary facilities. Furnishes surety bond, when requested.	
OTHER CONTRACTOR RESPONSIBILITIES	Specifies nominal completion date, and "outside date" for absolute completion. Responsible for correct supervision and execution of work. Responsible for defects due to labor and material for at least 1 yr., also for damage caused by his negligence. Have house spotlessly clean, ready for occupancy.	
OWNER RESPONSIBILITIES		To meet all payments as might be specified and stipulated between owner and contractor. Not to interfere with contractor's working policies, and to have all changes and change orders in written agreement.

To avoid misunderstandings, everything agreed upon between contractor and owner should be reduced to writing and included in the General Contract. All promises, obligations, and duties of contractor and owner to each other should be specifically stated.

Where there is an architect, his duties in relation to those of the contractor should also be set forth.

A description of all materials and their quality, work to be performed, and trades to be employed, as well as plans and specifications, should be incorporated into the General Contract.

FINANCIAL ARRANGEMENTS: OWNER-CONTRACTOR

There are several different business arrangements under which contractors will build a home, but no matter what method is agreed upon, exact terms should be set down in the General Contract. As the owner, you must be sure of your financial arrangements, so, no commitments are made which cannot be kept, in full, at the designated time.

LUMP SUM CONTRACTS is the method used when a contractor submits a bid, agreeing to build a house for a set sum, including all cost and profit. The owner pays this one amount, plus any specific "extras."

COST PLUS CONTRACT is where the contractor is paid the actual cost of materials and labor, plus a specified fee for overhead and profits. The fee is an agreed percentage usually ranging from 10 to 15 per cent of total home cost.

PARTIAL PAYMENTS are often used under cost-plus contracts, when the owner is paying from his own funds, or when a construction loan is available. Sometimes these payments are made monthly, but, more often, are made in accordance with building stages. For instance, a set payment (usually cost, less 10 per cent) is made when the foundation is laid; another payment, when the building is framed; another when the frame is roofed and enclosed; still another when plumbing, wiring, and heating installation have been roughed in; another when plastering is done; and a final payment when the building is accepted for occupancy.

ON COMPLETION CONTRACT usually used in buying a project-type home, means merely that the contractor accepts the usual deposit, then receives full payment at the closing, when the entire house is completed and is accepted by the owner.

OWNER-CONTRACTOR RELATIONSHIP

Basically, in the process of building your home, the contractor furnishes all material and performs all work for the job. He is directly responsible for:

1. Fulfillment of all provisions and terms of the contract.
2. Ordering, purchasing, examining, receiving materials.
3. Coordinates movement of material to building site, to insure building schedule does not suffer from lack of available material.
4. Awards sub-contracts for specific work, scheduling these operations for smooth, efficient production.
5. Directs, inspects and maintains responsibility for work.

Since contracts are binding on both parties, each having specific obligations, the contractor expects you to:

1. Meet payments as scheduled in the contract.
2. Not to interfere with his scheduling of work or purchase of materials. (You have no right, simply because a relative sells lumber, to insist that the contractor buy from him.)
3. Should you decide on a change or alteration in your original plans, the contractor must have them in writing, and specifications and plans must be altered to conform to changes.
4. Should you have suggestions, or complaints, they are to be made to the contractor—not to his workers or sub-contractors. Since the contractor is responsible for the work, he is the only one authorized to give orders. He

will welcome your interest, but, for obvious reasons, he cannot tolerate interference with his schedules or his smooth working operations.

THE CLOSING

The closing is the final step in negotiations for your new home. A final inspection should be made of the house immediately prior to this vital meeting, and, if there are errors or omissions in the work or construction, these discrepancies should be brought out at the closing. Complaints will be discussed among you, the builder, and the lending institution. If complaints are legitimate, the lending institution will probably hold sufficient money in escrow until everything is corrected to meet contract terms. By holding out some of the settlement money, the lending institution can either force the builder to correct defects, or to use such funds to pay someone else to do the work—should the builder refuse. Small complaints, such as sticking windows, a few missing nails, etc., can be ironed out on a friendly basis between you and the builder—but an agreement should be reached before the closing.

A CERTIFICATE OF OCCUPANCY should be turned over to you by the builder, certifying that the local building and health departments have examined the house and proclaimed it a healthy, safe place to live in. He should also provide certificates stating that adequate plumbing, electrical and sanitary facilities, which meet local codes and requirements, will be properly installed.

All GUARANTEES and WARRANTIES pertaining to your home should be supplied by the contractor at closing time. Manufacturer's guarantees for the roof, heating plant, air conditioning, range and oven, refrigerator, and any other mechanical equipment, should be turned over to you before final payment is made to the builder. Your attorney should have sufficient time before the closing to examine these guarantees and warranties for sufficiency.

WAIVER OF LIENS, covering all materials, sub-contracts, and other work, should be turned over by the builder at the time of settlement. In lieu of individual waivers, or receipted bills, a <u>blanket waiver of lien</u> should be executed in your favor by the contractor. Under a Partial Payment Plan, waivers of liens should be presented upon each payment, covering material and work up to that point. At the closing, any material and work, not as yet covered, should be certified in waiver of lien form by the Contractor. This is your insurance against having a labor lien filed later by a disgruntled sub-contractor, or a repossession order lodged against your appliances by an unpaid dealer.

The closing is your last chance to register any dissatisfactions or complaints. When you accept the deed, you acknowledge that everything is to your satisfaction and that the contractor has completely and faithfully discharged his contract with you. This authorizes the lending institution to pay the contractor in full. If you have exceptions or complaints, make sure that they are specifically noted and covered by escrow money. Only when everything has been done to your <u>complete satisfaction</u>, should you accept title to, and move into, the home.

Chapter 3

SELECTING YOUR BUILDING LOT

The question of whether to choose the lot before planning the house—or vice versa—has been a problem for almost as long as the ancient question: which came first, the chicken or the egg. However, the pattern most successfully used by veteran architects and builders is to plan both of them together. Unless you know the type of home you will build, selection of the lot will be extremely difficult—and perhaps an expensive mistake.

Actually, the type of home you contemplate building will have considerable bearing on the size, shape, and location of the land. Contours of the lot that would be a definite hazard or eyesore for one type of construction may be exactly what is needed for another type.

When you buy a lot with the intention of building your home on it, you not only acquire a piece of land; you literally purchase a share in a neighborhood. Since you will doubtless live in the chosen location for many years, considerable care and thought should go into your final selection. While building experts usually hold that 15 per cent of the home's total cost is normal for the lot, the actual cash expenditure is secondary to whether or not you will be happy living in that community.

NEIGHBORHOOD

Select a neighborhood with a high percentage of homeowners, and observe the condition of homes and buildings. Homes in the area should be of comparative value to the amount you intend investing, since it is seldom possible to recover cost for a house that is more expensive than the average house in that area. If surrounding homes are not maintained in good condition, or if the over-all appearance of the area is not attractive, it might be wise to look elsewhere. The neighborhood, which is the greatest single influence on the market value of a home, also plays an important part in regard to mortgage terms, and is of prime concern in preserving re-sale value.

While close access to shopping centers, churches, schools and playgrounds is desirable, you don't want them so close that you will be annoyed by the traffic flow. You will also wish to be within close proximity to public transportation, but not on highways or heavily traveled roads, which present a noise problem as well as a hazard to safe playing for children. The neighborhood should not be situated in the path of commercial or industrial growth, and should be zoned for residential structures only.

Spend a few hours walking around, talking to people. Find out if they are friendly, what their impression is of that community, whether or not they regret having located there. Particularly, talk to people living near the lot you contemplate buying, since they will be your neighbors, if you decide to build there. Also, talk to homeowners several lots away, since they often give information that might be withheld by persons directly next door.

Make inquiries as to why that particular lot has remained unsold. If there are undesirable hidden factors, it's best you discover them before closing the deal. A building lot might be beautiful in summer, but inaccessible during the winter months. Zoning may have made the lot so restricted that it is almost worthless. There might be a solid rock ledge, only a few inches below surface, that would make building prohibitively expensive. It will pay to be suspicious of any lot that has remained unsold for any length of time; if it appeals to you, it must also have appealed to others—why didn't they buy it?

GRADING

One of the first factors that should be determined is whether or not the lot has adequate natural drainage. It should be sufficiently graded to drain water away from the house in all directions, and carry it completely away from the lot. Figure

Selecting Your Building Lot

a minimum ground slope of 1 inch to every 10 feet for adequate drainage. Where a house will have to be situated below street level, you are in danger of a moisture condition around the foundation—and possibly in your basement.

Freshly filled land should receive careful inspection. Unless the fill has been complete, well packed, and has had time to "settle," you might encounter heavy additional building expenses. Special piling or "spread footing" may be needed on filled land to prevent uneven settling of the house; and while these construction modifications will serve the purpose, <u>they add considerably to building costs</u>.

A high, rocky site can also present several problems. This can mean added cost of mass excavation—quite expensive in hard or rocky ground—or, if the rock is generalized throughout the lot, it could also mean you will be unable to have a garden or trees.

Sloping lots are ideal for split-level construction, but, again, you could be faced with heavy excavation bills, if the slope is too great. Figure a maximum slope for grass banks at about 1 foot vertical to 4 feet horizontal; with approximately 1 foot in 10 for gardens. If you plan a ranch or Cape Cod house, a sloping lot problem may add up to several thousand dollars for either blasting or filling the land.

A North slope is cool in summer. A South slope offers protection from wintry north winds, but it catches direct, hot sun rays in summer. For this reason the climate of your area should enter into your final decision in selecting a lot.

Give surrounding lots a close view when considering the drainage problem, especially if adjacent lots are higher than the one you plan to buy. In such a case, you can suspect that water drained from them will deluge the property you are considering—which could present a serious, expensive problem should you build on the lower lot. Before making a final decision on any building lot, make a special inspection trip on a rainy day to observe how the existing grade handles natural drainage. Even if it means waiting several weeks for a heavy rain, it is better to wait than to have a flooded basement for years to come.

LOT SHAPE

Generally, a square or rectangular lot is most desirable. While an odd shaped lot may provide extra frontage, it will probably create a cramped condition in the rear. "Crazy lots," (as odd shaped parcels are called by real estate men) often provide interesting architectural possibilities, providing they are sufficiently large. Unless you contemplate an individual design compatible with a large, odd-shaped lot, you will probably be much happier with a lot of conventional size and shape.

SOIL CHECK

Before buying an unimproved piece of land, a "percolation test" should be made to determine the moisture-absorbing qualities of the earth. This is particularly important in areas where septic tank systems are used, since the system will not function properly in hard clay or in non-porous soil. The surface may appear quite normal in absorption, but there could be a thick layer of hardpan (a rock or clay layer just a few inches under the top fill). A "perk test" consists of digging a series of holes in the ground, filling them with water, then clocking the absorption time.

Many communities will not issue an occupancy permit on homes having septic tank systems until a "perk test" has been made <u>and recorded</u>. This test is not of great importance where municipal sanitary sewer systems are available, but it can be the basis upon which you decide upon the landscape for that lot.

Where there is reason to suspect that a rock ledge might be running through the lot, it is advisable to drill holes, about 4 feet deep, in a criss-cross pattern. Where builders run into rock ledges the cost of excavation can increase several thousand dollars. The auger holes may also reveal the presence of shale formations which can hold back water and cause wet basements —even on hill tops. By the same token, if auger testing reveals quicksand, peat or marl conditions, building costs will probably be increased by at least a thousand dollars for the concrete pilings and grade beams required to stabilize such conditions.

Selecting Your Building Lot

LANDSCAPING

Check to determine whether the soil is sufficiently fertile to have a garden, or whether you will have to buy topsoil and fertilizer. Little added expenses such as these can wreck a carefully planned building budget. At this point you must also take into consideration the question of a large lawn, which, each year, will require many hours of hard work.

It is desirable to have a few trees on your building lot. Strategically placed trees provide beauty and comfort, while reducing heating and air-conditioning costs over the years. If you must decide among several lots, give preferred thought to the one that has trees of the evergreen and deciduous variety. Planting trees after the house is built may be expensive, and, usually, years are required for the trees to mature to the point where they will actually service your home.

YOUR WATER SUPPLY

When contemplating the purchase of a lot that will not be serviced by a regular, municipal water supply, a test should be made to determine the availability of well water. Water is frequently located at 10 or 12 feet, but sometimes you may have to drill to a depth of 100 or 150 or more feet before suitable water is found. The difference in depth can mean that hundreds of dollars will be added to your building costs. However, water found close to ground level is often polluted; it is advisable to have water samples from that property, or from nearby property, tested by the state health department. Determine, also, if the water is extremely hard (or loaded with mineral or chemicals). In such cases water-softener units will probably be required—which will add a few hundred dollars to your building costs.

MUNICIPAL FACILITIES

Before you decide to buy a particular lot, check the municipal facilities of that area. Pay special attention to whether the locality has adequate police and fire portection. This provides safer living for you and your family, and adequate protection is also a determining factor in fire and burglary insurance rates. If proper protection is not available, you can expect higher insurance premiums—and, later, should such service be added, a rise in your tax rates.

Check closely to determine whether water, gas, electricity and sewage are available—and whether rates for these services are within reason. Another point to investigate is whether or not there is a municipal trash and garbage collection—or would you have to pay extra for such facilities?

PROPERTY LINES

A contract might call for a building lot of 80 by 150 feet, but it will require a survey to find out if this footage <u>actually</u> exists—and just where the property lines begin and end. When you arrive at the point of the <u>closing</u>, it will be wise to have a survey made—unless lot markers have already been posted by a recent survey. At the time of settlement, insist upon receiving a surveyor's report from the seller, which clearly establishes your property lines. If such a report doesn't exist, perhaps you can have the seller pay for one, or, at least, split the cost with you. Normally, a survey of an average lot will cost less than fifty dollars.

A misunderstanding about just a few feet might necessitate moving your house in later years, should it develop that a "guess" at property lines was wrong, and you have built on—or too near—someone else's property. Especially in suburban and rural areas, many original deeds establish property lines by "the North side of Jones's Creek," or "10 feet beyond the big Oak." But that creek might have dried up, or changed course, or the "Big Oak" could have been stricken by blight many years ago. The adage of "an ounce of prevention," very definitely applies to defining the location of <u>true</u> property lines.

Selecting Your Building Lot

ZONING LAWS AND BUILDING CODES

Primarily, zoning laws and building codes are designed to assist and protect home and land owners. For instance, a lot in an outlying location, unprotected by zoning, might be reasonable in price, but since there are no zoning restrictions a junk yard or fat rendering plant could be built next to it.

Full explanations of zoning laws and building codes are available in town and city halls. In some localities copies may be purchased, or are supplied free, so that they may be studied at home. Zoning laws will determine the minimum footage you must own to build a home, plus how much of the lot may be covered by the building, and how far the house must be set back from the street line, side lines, and rear boundary lines of the property.

Zoning laws may stipulate a minimum square footage of living space a one-story house must contain; or, they might forbid construction altogether of one-story or split-level homes in certain areas. They might also determine what type of garage you can erect on the property, and how it must be situated; or, the laws may specify the type and height of fences, or whether you can build a swimming pool, and the maximum height for your TV antenna.

Zoning laws will also cover such matters as your being allowed to have roomers or boarders. They may even have a restriction against having a professional office in your home. While all this may sound grim, these same laws maintain your property values, since they protect you against invasion of undesirable commercial or factory buildings, inferior residential structures, and other community eye-sores that would detract from your home and property.

Building Codes are usually administered on a local level, by village, town or city officials. They set forth minimum standards of construction for that locality, specifying building materials and methods proved from safety and soundness standpoints. The codes will, for instance, set a minimum thickness for foundations, minimum strength of lumber used in construction, minimum standards and prescribed methods of installing electrical wiring and the plumbing. Sanitation standards are set forth, beginning with the plumbing and water level, to determine the maximum number of people who may occupy a certain amount of living space.

While these restrictions may sound arbitrary, they are designed for your protection, as well as that of the entire community. They would, for example prevent an unscrupulous builder from using inferior material in your home, or keep indiscriminate people from operating a cheap rooming house next to you (which would depreciate your property overnight). Most people with reasonable plans and expectations for their homes will find that zoning and building restrictions do little to hinder them but, on the contrary, go a long way toward protecting their investment in the community.

Subdivision restrictions are controlled by developers of subdivisions, or, in some cases, by the neighborhood common council. In keeping with the atmosphers of the community, there might be restrictions against building any type of home other than one of contemporary design, or, if all the homes in that subdivision are of the ranch type, there might be a restriction against tri-level, or larger, homes that would overshadow lower buildings. In all probability there will be a minimum value set for new building. Some subdivisions restrict the removal of trees over eight inches in diameter, without prior permission from the developer or neighborhood association; or they prohibit the removal of soil without approval. These deed restrictions are valid, <u>and can be enforced,</u> so investigate carefully before making a final decision on buying a lot.

TAXES AND ASSESSMENTS

Pay close attention to whether "off-side improvements" such as storm sewers, paved streets, curbs, and gutters, etc., have been provided and paid for—or whether you will later be assessed for them. Depending on the frontage of the lot, these improvement assessments can run to sizeable figures. If your investigation shows that such assessments will be made in the near future, determine an approximate expense for that particular lot, and consider such extra money in the overall price.

Especially in growing communities, find out whether taxes

Selecting Your Building Lot

have risen appreciably within recent years, and how much tax you will pay there. In some localities, a home may be subject to several taxes—such as village, town, and county assessments. Check with each assessor for a full view of all taxation.

New communities faced with "growing pains," frequently take on large debts for schools, fire and police protection, water and sewage systems, roads and streets, all of which are pro-rated into tax assessments against property owners. Government bodies have no regard for upsetting individual budgets—they are only interested in collecting money to liquidate their debts—even if it means putting individual property owners in the red.

EASEMENTS AND RIGHTS-OF-WAY

Check with the appropriate municipal agency, and through the title and abstracts, as to the existence of any rights-of-way or easements on the property, for utility lines, drains, rights for neighboring properties to draw from the water supply of that property, or numerous other situations that might late prove undesirable.

Michigan courts recently ruled against a property owner who belatedly discovered that the county had a drainage easement on his land. Since he hadn't bothered checking into this important phase, he blissfully built a cottage, sank a 90-foot well and laid an expensive septic tank system—all utilizing some of the easement area. When a serious drainage problem made it necessary for the county to exercise easement, and caused removal of the man's house, well, and septic system, he was annoyed. But even righteous indignation doesn't compensate for failure to maintain easements.

In suburban and rural areas, be particularly alert to old rights-of-way that may be included in the title. What is now suburban was "countryside" only a few years ago, and there may be rights-of-way for roads running directly through that property. Even if the right-or-way is never exercised, you might be unable, later, to sell the land because of such restrictions. Again, the "ounce of prevention" is worth may pounds of cure—therefore, check first, so you won't be sorry later.

CONDEMNATION

Before reaching the settlement stage, when buying a building lot, check through the City Planning Commission for any foreseeable condemnation possibilites. You will be wise to check in all four directions from the lot for possible extension of expressways or highways that might cross the property in the near future. Find out who owns the land on either side of your lot, as this can often be a clue to the future. Where such adjacent land is owned by a railroad, hospital, church or governmental agency, their future plans should be investigated.

PROFESSIONAL ASSISTANCE

Real estate <u>brokers</u> usually charge 10 per cent for their services, but unless you have a definite property in mind, this might be a wise investment. A well established broker knows many little factors about neighborhoods, future plans of areas, etc., that work to your advantage. He will generally give excellent advice, since his clientele of tomorrow, depends upon his satisfied clients of today. If you are going to employ an architect or builder for your new home, have them evaluate the lot before closing the deal.

Don't buy a lot unless you intend building in the near future. Many things can happen to a neighborhood over a period of a few years that might make unimproved property lose value. Public tastes can change, with the trend, in a few years, being toward the other side of town, or toward differently shaped lots. Or, a few years might make such a difference in your thinking that the lot which looks good today, might not appeal to you—or fit in with your plans—several years from now.

From the economy standpoint an empty lot produces no revenue, but taxes must still be paid. An empty lot will be assessed as much as improved property if the municipal authorities decide to install roads, sewers, etc. Perhaps other people will also allow their lots to remain unimproved, which will depreciate the value of your land. An empty lot can become what is known a as an "attractive nuisance," if children are drawn to it as a playground; and—to top it all—if anyone should suffer an injury from crossing your empty lot or playing on it, you will be liable for damages.

Make your plans for buying the lot and constructing your home at the same time. Your decision in both the lot selection and home design will be much better because of the consolidated thinking.

Chapter 4

PROPERLY ORIENT YOUR HOME

Proper positioning of a house on the lot can result, over the years, in a savings of thousands of dollars in immediate construction costs and in light, heat and air conditioning bills. It can also make the difference between enjoying your home and ground 24 hours a day, or having a nasty situation wherein some areas are uncomfortable during certain hours—or for the entire season.

Boiled down to basic facts, when a house is scientifically positioned, intelligently landscaped, with sufficient glass in the right places, and has adequate overhang on the roof, nature will help make the home more comfortable, livable, economical.

Improper positioning of the house is probably the most common, costly mistake made in home planning today. For good site planning, it is necessary first to break the lot into three different zones; public, service and private:

THE PUBLIC ZONE is the strip of land that borders along the front sidewalk. By eliminating alleys, modern community planning has made the approach to the house a public area, directing all access to the house from the street. Zoning regulations usually specify how far back the house must be placed on the lot, but ordinarily there is no reason to make this area larger. The old type "front yard" with its display of lawn, has yielded to larger private areas designed for family enjoyment and privacy.

THE SERVICE ZONE, or utility area, if well placed and planned, need not be large. This area should be accessible to walks and driveway so that deliveries may be made to the service door without intrusion upon the private area. The garage which should be adjacent to the service area, should have storage space for garden tools and other equipment.

THE PRIVATE ZONE is the outdoor living space for the family. Unlike the "back yard" of yesteryear, it is planned for pleasant recreational activities for the entire family. An expanse of

Properly Orient Your Home

lawn, or garden, a porch or terrace, barbecue pit or play-yard, are most commonly included in this area.

Common sense dictates using the least possible amount of valuable land for public and service use, with the maximum amount devoted to private enjoyment. This includes the house being set as far forward on the lot as is practical, in keeping with the local zoning regulations. In many cases, fullest utilization of the lot is obtained from houses oriented toward the rear, with the house screening the private zone from the public streets.

By locating as close to the street as possible, you save through short and economical driveways and walks which require a minimum maintenance—not to mention snow clearance. The distance that utility pipes and wires must run from the street to the house will also be minimized, with resultant, substantial cash savings to your building budget. *(See illustration page 84)*

PROPER HOME ORIENTATION

A home properly oriented in relation to the sun has Nature working with it all year round. By capitalizing on the sun's full factors, fuel bills can be reduced up to 40 per cent, rooms will receive maximum sunshine (requiring less artificial light), and the house can be 10 degrees or more cooler during the summer months.

It has been scientifically proved that, primarily because the path of sun travel varies daily, the south side of a house receives approximately 5 times as much sun heat in winter as in summer; the west and east sides receive 6 times as much sun heat in summer as in winter; while the north side receives no solar heat during winter months. The summer sun will reach a high angle of about 73 degrees on June 21st, diminishing to about 50 degrees as the season wanes. During the summer months, the sun will rise in the northeast, travel a high arc, and set in the northwest. In the winter, it rises in the southeast and sets in the southwest. The secret of good house orientation is to locate so that you may take maximum advantage of this seasonal situation, and let Nature work with you.

Since houses that face due south will receive the most direct

sunshine in winter, and the least in summer, it is usually desirable to have the main living area and largest windows face directly south. Depending upon the lot location, this could mean facing the house away from the street, with the private zone in the rear, or having the side of the house parallel to the public street. Although people have fallen into the habit of facing their homes towards the public street, zoning laws in most communities will allow a house to be positioned in the manner most desirable to the owner. So don't just place your home toward the street for convention's sake, and then find out that you are losing Nature's help in heating and cooling.
(See illustration page 92)

HEATING

A home with large glassed areas facing north or west, will be subject to heavy heating bills. This is because even double-layer glass, with its "dead air space," doesn't effectively insulate from cold winds, and so, heat is lost. Windows facing east will admit sun heat during the early morning hours, but will also allow house heat to escape during the balance of the day.

Large windows, in the southern portion of the house, unaffected by cold winter winds, capture the maximum amount of natural sun heat during the day. With sufficient sun heat entering through large window areas, the house can be kept warm even on cold days, without an additional heat source. Heavy drapes on southern windows should be opened during the morning hours to admit the friendly, warm sun, but closed during the evening, to retain the heat captured during the day.

Evergreen trees, planted along the northern portion of the lot line, provide a natural shield against ravaging winter winds and drifting snow. Where such trees are not practical, icy winds may be controlled by situating the garage as a buffer, north or northwest of the house. *(See illustration page 86)*

COOLING

Unless control measures are employed, the same sunshine that helps heat your home during winter months, will make it unbearable in summer. Having the sun in the winter, but not in the summer, parallels the situation of having your cake and eating it, but it can be done.

Because the summer sun rides high, a wide roof overhang provides shade for the windows, deflecting direct heat rays. Such an overhang will not interfere with the free solar heat of winter months, since the winter sun shines in at a much lower angle than the summer sun.

Ideally, the house should be situated east of tall deciduous trees, which become a cooling barrier between the afternoon sun and the house. They also prove invaluable when the summer sun sinks in the afternoon, and its rays hit the western part of the house, on an almost horizontal line. Without shade tree protection, west walls will absorb a phenomenal amount of heat from the setting summer sun. The walls literally become radiant heat panels, dissipating the stored up heat into west rooms during the night. If these trees are of the deciduous type, their foliage will fall in conjunction with winter's approach, and the bare branches won't interfere with the rays of the setting sun, supplying free heat.

The same trees, used for sun ray blocking, should be situated so as to add summer comfort by shading the house's roof. The cooler you keep attic and roof, the quicker heat will rise from within, lowering the temperature in your living areas.

Where it is impractical to place trees on the west side of the house, the garage, positioned here, will frequently act as a barrier against setting summer sun rays, but will usually not interfere with the desirable setting winter sun's heat.

(See illustration page 89)

BREEZES

By taking advantage of cool northern breezes in summer, you can make your home more comfortable, and take a heavy load off your air conditioning system. Curving evergreen hedges, north and east, will trap and circulate cool summer breezes around the house and grounds, providing pleasant evenings on the patio. The same bank of evergreens will act as an effective windbreak in winter, to stand off icy northern winds and drifting snow.

Oversize louvers in the north and west walls of the attic will also keep the attic "air-washed," and help to cool rooms below. These extra large louvers should be in addition to the regular ventilation openings, so that they can be closed in winter, with just the regular vents open enough for circulation to prevent winter condensation. By letting Nature help cool your home, you will save money on the original installation cost of all air conditioning equipment, as well as operating expenses through the years.

NATURAL LIGHT

The kitchen, dinette and laundry areas, forming the center of daytime activity, require the most sunlight. Electric bills can be appreciably reduced, and more pleasant living conditions provided, if these much-used rooms are on the south side of the house, where the sun provides a maximum of free, natural light.

HOUSE AND GARDEN AS A UNIT

Landscape planning should begin when the original scheme for your home is being considered—not after it is built. In laying out the lot design, preserve natural resources such as trees, original native plants, good soil, etc. When a landscape specialist is used, have him collaborate with your architect, right from the beginning.

The smaller the house, ground and budget, the greater the need for correct and complete planning, since every square foot of space and every dollar must be made to produce maximum results. Plan for complete landscaping, even though you actually spread the development over a period of years to pro-rate the work and expense. Keep in mind that complicated landscaping requires constant maintenance. If you are not the type who enjoys working in the garden, plan for minimum upkeep. The best lawn design is a smooth area, simple in shape, unobstructed. And since you have to mow the lawn, avoid steep banks or cluttered arrangements which cause extra work and effort.

TREES

If you are fortunate enough to find a lot with trees, they should play an important role in your house planning. It is expensive having trees cut down and hauled away; even more expensive to discover later that you must plant new trees for proper shading and wind protection. A little thought in the initial planning stage might save hundreds of dollars, and provide ideal living conditions, through utilization of existing trees. In calculating the sun and wind protection needed for your house, consider the buffering effects you will derive from trees and buildings on neighboring lots.

Best results are obtained from wide spreading deciduous trees, positioned off the corners of the house. Overplanting, with trees too close together, shuts out both air circulation and sunlight. Trees may be considered well-positioned when their adjoining tops just meet, in full foliage.

PATIO AND TERRACE

The most comfortable location for a patio or terrace is north of the house, where it will be in the house shadows most of the day, yet still have cool northern breezes during the evening. Play areas for children should be far enough away from the house so that noise will not disturb those inside, and the building won't block off direct sun rays, essential to children. If your family enjoys patio breakfasts, such facilities should be planned for the northeast corner so that you can enjoy the rising sun. The northwest corner provides best conditions for a late afternoon use of terrace or patio, since it will receive the most effects from the setting sun.

PLUMBING AND WATER

The house should be situated on an elevated part of the lot for good drainage. When a septic tank system is used, it should be located as close as possible to the public street, which will involve a minimum of expense when you eventually hook up to public sewage.

Considerable money can also be saved by locating the house close to the street line, where public drainage and water supply systems are available. In estimating water supply and disposal lines, cost is figured on the length of pipe run required from the main water supply, or waste lines, to the house. On a large-sized lot, you can save hundreds of dollars by building close to main lines, eliminating long pipe runs. Short pipe runs not only mean substantial savings in construction, but present you with less maintenance and repair problems throughout the year.

Regardless of lot size, construction and plumbing supply costs can be reduced if you plan the house with all water consuming rooms, such as kitchen, bathrooms, laundry, etc., on the side of the house nearest the water and sewage lines.

CLOSING

When it comes time for building, remember that builders have the right to use only that part of the land needed for construction operations. Restrict them from defacing the rest of the lot. During construction, protect existing trees, roots and surrounding shrubs by building rough wooden fences or shields around them, if necessary.

Your neighbors also have the right to protection from your buildings, so have this definitely understood from the beginning. Also, have a clear agreement that odds and ends of building material (lime, building paper, wood-ends, shavings, etc.) are to be removed from the premises—not buried in the ground, as contractors often do. Burying the debris will not be conducive to growing plants—or even a good stand of grass—and small pockets of wood buried in the ground will provide breeding grounds for destructive termites.

Chapter 5

HOW TO BUY AN EXISTING HOME

Three million single family homes are sold in the United States each year. Most of the new homeowners are well-satisfied, consider their purchase a good investment, feel their dreams have come true. Others are destined for headaches, heartaches and bills, with the house constituting a liability, the dreams taking on the quality of nightmares. The difference between the good and bad investment, the beautiful dream and the nightmare, lies in being alerted, before the contract is signed, for major faults and hidden expenses.

Whether you purchase a new or an older house, total sales price must be computed to include the "extra" charges, or expenses, plus the cost of the house. Knowing the pitfalls and precautions to look for in both new and old homes, you'll find, will make a big difference in the amount you spend, the value you receive, the comfort you derive from the house after you take possession.

Generally, the year an older house was built will provide a clue to its quality. Houses built during the 1920's were structurally sound, but mechanically deficient in heating, plumbing and wiring. Building improved during the 1930's—particularly following the creation of the FHA in 1934. By 1940, builders began using copper and brass pipe, automatic heating and rock lath. From 1941 to 1946, houses were basically designed for temporary housing, because of World War II, and rationed materials were frequently substituted with the result that people ended up with inferior structures. From 1947 on, construction improved steadily and better houses were built. However, there will naturally be some exceptions to the above general conditions, so don't condemn a house just because it was built during a specific year. A detailed check of a house—whether new or old— is the only way you can be sure of getting what you want for the amount you are able, or willing, to spend.

GENERAL CONDITIONS

Inspect as much house framing as possible to determine whether or not seasoned lumber was used. Green, unseasoned lumber shrinks and warps as moisture content changes, often causing structural weakness and deterioration. In new houses, less than a year old, it will probably be difficult to detect the total damaging effects of green lumber. "Popped nails," cracked plaster, open trim joints, boards pulled away from mountings, all are warning signs of improperly seasoned lumber's having been used. Loose or buckled wallboard also indicates use of green lumber, and repairs will entail renailing, retaping, replastering and painting—which, as you can readily see—will be an expensive proposition.

An occasional broken, warped, or rotted shingle or clapboard is easily replaced at small expense. Widespread deterioration, if it is due to normal weathering, is not harmful, but such a condition will call for new siding, which is costly. Extensive rot in a house less than 20 years old may be due to improper paint, interior moisture, or to other serious defects, and should be considered a potentially dangerous, costly warning against that particular property.

Small cracks in plaster are neither unusual nor harmful. Long, deep ones are probably caused by structural defects that doubtless will become progressively worse. Cracked plaster, where walls meet ceilings, is generally caused by excessive expansion and contraction of wall-studding plates. Such cracks could be caused by green lumber, or, when found on the second level, by a poorly ventilated attic. Where flooring has pulled away from baseboards, it is often necessary to pull up the entire floor for corrective work—an expensive job. Squeaking and creaking floors announce that poor nailing technique has been used, green lumber has warped and pulled loose, or uneven settling of the building has pulled structural members apart. A close check should be made to determine the exact cause, and the amount of damage.

How to Buy an Existing Home   45

Consistent settling of a house can be easily and quickly checked with any perfectly round object, such as a ball, a child's marble, a bearing, etc., simply by placing the round object in the center of the floor and noting its speed as it rolls. A slight slant is to be expected in most houses—but be extremely cautious of any house which has settled to one side.

Inspect all windows and doors for ease of operation as you open and close them. This is one of the first places uneven building settling will be noticed. Also examine storm doors, windows and screens. Frequently these seasonal accessories are stored improperly, are thus subject to rapid deterioration, and are costly to replace.

FOUNDATION

No structure is more durable and strong than the foundation upon which it stands. Building codes and municipal inspections generally supervise and control foundation construction and soil density factors; however, since this is such an important part of a house, a personal check is advisable.

Usually, footings should be at least 6 inches below frost line, 8 inches thick and 16 inches wide for a one- or a one-and-a-half story house; 12 inches thick and 24 inches wide for two-story houses. In a case where ground has been heavily filled, or the earth is unstable, larger footings are required. A concrete block foundation should have a top course of solid blocks, or two courses of regular blocks, core holes of which are filled with concrete. Concrete slab foundations should be at least 4 inches thick, reinforced with rods or wire mesh, and should rest on a 4 inch bed of gravel or crushed stone. There should also be a moisture barrier between slab and gravel of at least a 55 lb. roll roofing, or material equivalent in durablity and vapor resistance. Check these figures with the Real Estate Broker, builder or Inspector.

If the foundations of a house are inadequate, uneven settling will frequently be encountered. If footings on slab and basementless homes are not placed below frost lines, moisture freezes beneath the concrete, causing heaving and twisting.

Then, the walls, rigidly held by framing, develop horizontal cracks in plaster and outside masonry, because of the heaving and the uneven settling.

Thin masonry cracks and open mortar joints are warning signs which should be investigated. They could be relatively harmless superficial cracks, or they might mean big trouble. Check for cracked plaster extending diagonally across inside walls from corner of doors and windows; this is usually a warning of uneven settling. Such signs could mean extremely expensive repairs—if, indeed, repair should be possible—so, have a qualified person investigate such findings.

Where foundation walls are of insufficient strength, the weight of surrounding soil alone can cause cracks. Water, freezing in the ground against a weak foundation, will cause horizontal cracking at grade line, or halfway up. So again, proceed cautiously where such signs are found. Wherever cracks are located, have a specialist check the property before closing the deal.

BASEMENT

Because structural members such as beams, joists, subflooring, cross members and foundation walls can be examined, the basement usually lends itself to a good insight into a house. Examine all visible structural members for signs of dry rot, mildew, poor fitting, termites and green lumber. Check rotted looking areas with a thin knife blade or an ice pick. An occasional soft spot in old joists or beams is not fatal, but if the blade penetrates several inches, the members are defective and will have to be replaced. If many joists or beams are affected in this manner, you might be wise to forget that particular house.

Give close attention, especially to wood ceiling structure directly over the heating unit. Where green lumber has been used, this will be the first area affected by warping. Warped or shrunken beams cause upstairs plaster walls to crack, and create a generally poor structure. Floor bulges and cracks are also a sign of poor construction, and can be costly to repair. There should be rows of 1" x 3" cross bridging (X braces nailed between joists) to stiffen the joists, with rows no more than 8 feet apart. All beams should be positioned solidly into the walls. Some older houses have adjustable jack posts to shore up sagging joists, and these frequently used in small areas for support of heavy furniture or appliances, are a good indication of poor construction if they have been used to brace the entire floor.

Look carefully for high water marks in the basement and on walls, which indicate flooding conditions. Dark stains on walls or floors, or flaky wall cement, indicate water penetration. It can be a very expensive job to correct a wet basement, and should the fault be due to inadequate foundation, correction might be impossible unless you tore out the entire foundation. If there is a sump pump in the basement, it is usually a dead give-away that there is a serious water problem. The pump may be able to handle the flooding conditions, but it will preclude use of the basement for storage or living facilities, and the water will eventually take effect on the building's under-structure. If water penetration is serious enough to require sump pump action, the building will become progressively weaker, and such a house cannot be considered a good buy at any price. It is advisable, whenever a moisture condition is found, to have a competent builder completely investigate the cause before a contract is signed.

Where you are planning to use the basement as a living, storage, or recreation area, examine facilities cautiously. Determine whether or not there is sufficient ceiling height for you to stand erect and still have head room. If you plan to install flooring, or to finish the ceiling, this will lessen head room, so take such alterations into consideration. There should be an outside exit at least 36 inches wide, and sufficient windows and ventilation for healthy living conditions.

ROOF

With both new and old houses, insist upon the manufacturer's guarantee regarding the roof. On a new house, you can tell exactly what type and quality material has been used. On older houses the guarantee will give you the definite age of the material, and general present condition can be judged by the date of installation. Normally, in southern climates, the average asphalt shingle roof will last about 10 years; in northern climates, about 15 to 20 years. Desirably, asphalt shingles should be 250- to 300-pound material; however, 210- to 215-pound types are frequently acceptable under many building codes. A built-up roof, on a flat or low slope, usually requires repair or replacement within 15 years. Visually inspect for broken or missing shingles, and signs of extensive repair. Ragged, wrinkled, torn, or curled shingles are an indication that a new roof will soon be needed. A new asphalt shingle roof will cost from $400 to $700 for moderately sized homes, with proportionately higher prices for better material and larger roof areas.

Simple roofs, either flat or pitched, are the least costly to maintain. Except for necessary alterations in level and direction, avoid a roof that is cut up just for appearance's sake. Sight along the roof ridge. A sagging roof ridge must be considered a major structural fault—difficult and expensive to correct—and a sure sign of future trouble.

For the best dollar value, roof flashing should be of non-ferrous material, such as plastic, aluminum, copper, etc. Check gutters and downspouts for solid position and good condition. Rust spots and holes in gutters and spouts can usually be detected from the ground. If replacement is needed, figure at least $100 for galvanized material—considerably more for copper or aluminum. Wood gutters may look pretty, but they generally require more servicing and will probably not last as long. Some homes will not have gutters on roof edges; but this is no longer considered a fault in many modern structures if there is sufficient overhang and good drainage, and if gravel drain beds are installed around the entire house. However, if drainage is bad, you may have to add gutters, run offs, gravel drain beds, or dry wells, which will cost upwards of a hundred dollars more.

ATTIC

The attic is another good place to inspect, since many structural members are visible. All exposed timber should be carefully checked for wood rot, termites and proper joints. Inspect the ceilings, walls, and floor for tell-tale marks of water leaks, condensation, or excessive humidity. Adequate attic, or underroof ventilation is important for summer cooling and prevention of condensation in the winter. Where proper attic floor insulation exists, heat loss caused by ventilation will be incidental.

Preferably, floor joists should be 2" x 6" or larger. Where conventional raftered construction is used, beams should be provided on alternate rafters, while long span rafters should have additional support. Inspect the ceiling joists to see if they are lapped and nailed at intervals of at least every 4 feet, to tie rafter ends together. Check for wood rot in rafters. A single rafter can be replaced or strengthened, but extensive damage indicates serious leaks or a damaging moisture condition. When you are in doubt about sound structure, a professional inspection should be made.

Ceiling cracks along the bottom of attic knee walls indicate that the roof is not sufficiently rigid. If knee walls have been used to help support the roof, both the weight of winter snow, and wind pressure, will bear directly on joists under the knee walls. Look for cracked plaster at this point, which will indicate the need for expensive roof reinforcement.

If you plan on fully utilizing the attic, base your appraisal on whether there is sufficient space to allow for the attic's conversion into a living area. Be sure the stairway and entrance are adequate, and decide whether or not your proposed alterations are adaptable to the existing conditions.

INSULATION

Houses 15 years old, or older, almost invariably present an insulation problem. Most houses were built without insulation prior to 1940, but from that time until 1955 it was a generally accepted practice to use some insulation in attics, with little or no wall insulation. During World War II, when materials were hard to obtain, many builders again reverted to construction without insulation. Homes built since 1955 will probably have both wall and ceiling insulation, but they too should be checked to determine whether or not sufficient protection has been provided. In many instances, relatively new brick and masonry wall construction houses have been built without wall insulation, so look into this matter closely.

Improper insulation can add an additional cost of as much as 40 per cent to your heating and air-conditioning expenses. You should check this vitally important factor, for the insulation of an existing house will cost at least 25 cents per square foot of gross exterior wall area, plus at least 10 cents per square foot of attic floor surface. This could add another $250 to $500 to the total cost, depending on the size of the house. Check also for adequate weather-stripping and storm windows and doors. In cases where you will have to buy storm windows and doors, add several hundred dollars more to the total cost of the house.

In most cases attic floor insulation can be visually checked. Loose fill-type insulation is the cheapest, and is the type more likely to absorb moisture than batt or foil types which incorporate a moisture vapor barrier. When the attic is to be used as a living or general-use-area, insulation should also be installed in the roof. If possible, visit the house after a snow fall. If snow melts from its roof, while the surrounding houses still have visible snow on their roof surfaces, you can be reasonably sure the rapidly melting snow has been caused by an improper roof insulation's allowing valuable heat to escape. A visit to the house immediately after a heavy rain will also reveal leaks or moisture conditions that could otherwise be missed.

During the winter months, you can easily check wall insulation by holding your hand against the inside surface of an exterior wall, then holding the same hand against an interior partition wall. There should be little difference in temperature between the two wall surfaces. Where exterior walls are much colder, either inadequate insulation, or total lack of insulation, should be suspected. Until proper insulation is installed, such a house will be uncomfortable, even though it might be overheated.

A properly insulated home will have 6 inches of insulation under the roof, 3 inches in the walls, 2 inches under the floors. There should also be about 3 inches of perimeter insulation around the entire perimeter of concrete on houses that have concrete ground floors.

HEATING

A properly insulated, average sized house of 1,000 to 1,500 sq. ft. will cost from $150 to $200 a year to heat with oil—a little more to heat with gas. In buying an older house, ask to see previous heating bills. If they run substantially higher than they should, you would be wise to check into the cause before buying.

Generally, the age of a house is a good clue to potential heating system trouble. Heating units more than 25 years old often require extensive repair or replacement, particularly if the original coal furnace has been converted to oil or gas. Usually, a modern oil furnace, or gas fired one, with either forced-air or hot-water circulation, will be the best and least troublesome unit. Old gravity-air systems, or hand-fired coal units, are almost sure to cause trouble. Beware of old-fashioned radiant-heat units which require the tearing up of entire slabs whenever there is a leak—with resultant astronomical repair or replacement costs. If there is any suspicion of heating system inadequacy, have an experienced heating specialist look the system over carefully.

Determine whether the manufacturer's guarantee on the heating system, and on the hot water tank are still effective. Call the man who has been servicing the system, ask him what repairs have been made, what repairs may be needed in the near future, and how much such repairs will cost. Be sure the unit is of sufficient size for the house, and find out whether or not the system's ducts can be used jointly with air conditioning. Inspect the interior of the boiler and the furnace for signs of cracks, and check the exterior base of the unit for rust and general deterioration. Soot around a furnace, or a rumbling when it starts, are signs of a weak draft, and the installation of a blower may be necessary.

If possible, visit the house on a cold day. Turn the heat on, set the thermostat to 80 degrees, and listen for noises. Also, determine the length of time it takes for heat to reach the various rooms. A warm air unit should heat all parts of the house within 10 to 15 minuts, while a hot water system could take 30 minutes. A system is insufficient unless all rooms, particularly those on the second floor, are evenly and easily heated. If your plans call for heating the garage or attic, make sure the system is of sufficient capacity to accommodate such additional heating.

If a new heating unit is indicated, be cautious. The installation cost of a new warm-air furnace starts at $600, or better; the cost of a new hot water boiler may range from $750 to $1,500. Depending upon the type of unit and the size of the house, a completely new heating system can cost from $2,000 to $5,000.

PLUMBING

Perhaps the most frequent faults found in older houses are insufficient water pressure and inadequate plumbing facilities. This situation prevails almost invariably in houses more than 25 years old that have iron or steel pipes and fixtures. Brass, copper, and bronze pipes, which have a much longer life span, did not come into extensive use until about 1946, so they are seldom found in older homes. New homes should have copper plumbing and, if they don't, you can safely assume that the builder skimped on costs and, what's more, you'll probably discover other structural shortcomings. Carry a small magnet with you, for testing plumbing material. A magnet will give positive reaction to iron and steel, but it will not react to copper, brass, lead or other non-ferrous metal.

Turn on faucets full blast in the laundry, kitchen, and bathrooms, flushing the toilet at the same time. If there is adequate water pressure, there will be little difference from ordinary flow. Inadequate pressure will be evident if the flow from your upstairs faucets becomes notably decreased. Next, fill the tub, letting it drain as you flush the toilet; turn on sink faucets and allow the shower to run. An adequate drainage system will handle this mass flow, so if the water backs up, the system is insufficient.

Flush the toilet several times in quick succession. A cigarette tossed into the bowl should be completely carried away on a single flushing. A properly ventilated tank will empty, reseal, and shut off without noise or dripping. If there are two toilets, have them both checked simultaneously for water supply and drainage. This phase of your inspection should receive careful attention, because the business of installing a new pipe and fixture system can be an expensive, messy proposition.

Rundown domestic hot water storage tanks are found mostly in houses located in soft water areas where steel tanks are used. Minerals in water form a protective film on inside tank surfaces in hard water areas, but the same film formation reduces the openings of pipes, and this causes trouble. The recommended minimum capacity, for an average home, is a 40-gallon tank (but an 80-gallon minimum on electric hot water systems). Larger families, or houses of 3,000 sq. ft. or more, should have a tank twice the size of this minimum.

Where there is a septic tank system, find out which company has been serving it, and contact that company. Ask when the tank was last cleaned, inquire about the capacity and adequacy of the unit, the present condition, and whether additional costs are likely to be encountered within the immediate future. Septic tank repairs or new installations can run anywhere from $100 to $500.

ELECTRICAL

A recent survey of a thousand houses, 10 years old or older, revealed that 84 per cent had inadequate or improper service entrance and wiring. The older the house, the greater the chances that an additional or complete revision of the wiring system will be required. It is not unusual to find an absolute minimum service in entirely new development houses, and you will spend at least a hundred dollars bringing it up to the required service level.

Check wires leading into the house—there should be three of them. Old, two-wire systems are not sufficient for today's electrical demands. Then, examine the service entrance. The minimum recommended electrical capacity for a modern home is a three wire, 240 volt, 100 ampere service. In homes with electric ranges, electric heat, or where there is more than 3,000 sq. ft. of space, a 150 or 200 ampere service is recommended.

If you discover the house has only a 30 or 60 ampere service, figure from $300 to $600 or more into the sale price for new wiring. The cost will vary according to fixtures and installation involved, with accurate estimates from electrical contractors or utility companies suggested to ascertain the exact cost. Modern living demands an absolute minimum of from 8 to 10 circuits, with up to 20 circuits where there are numerous appliances, or in large houses. Generally, there should be a minimum of one convenience outlet for every 12 feet of wall, and for every 4 feet of counter space in the kitchen. The kitchen should also have separate outlets for the refrigerator and the stove, and enough duplex outlets to accommodate all appliances regularly used in kitchen operations. The number of branch circuits can be determined by counting the fuses in the box, as each circuit has a separate fuse.

If you contemplate installing air conditioning, driers, workshop or other heavy electrical equipment, this should be considered in your electrical survey, with cost of possible new lines included in the over-all price.

Light switches should be positioned at the entrance of each room, at the tops and bottoms of stairways, and at garage and basement doors. Bathroom switches should be near the door, but situated so that they cannot be reached by persons in the tub or shower. Check outside switches, sockets, and outlets to determine whether or not they are in good condition, and are waterproof.

PAINT

When paint is badly worn, but the base is still good, figure an additional $400 to $600 into the sale price for complete exterior painting. If the undercoating is poor, and the entire surface must be burned or scraped, add another $200 for preparation before painting.

In a case where there is flaking, peeling, cracking, or other defects, check to determine the extent and cause of such damage. Flaked or peeling paint generally develops from moisture underneath. This could mean building leaks which have resulted in moisture damage to the interior structure, and such repairs could be prohibitive if the condition has reached the stage where joists, studs, or beams need replacing. At best, the leaks will have to be corrected before new paint will hold, so add a proportionate amount in computing the <u>actual</u> sale price to compensate for such repairs.

Inspect closely around doors, windows, and other exterior openings—such as outside water faucets, where electrical wires enter the house, etc. All exterior surfaces should be sealed; if they aren't, a calking job is indicated—which will add another $50 to $100 to the total cost.

TERMITES

Termite damage and wood rot is generally found in houses more than 5 years old; however, infestation is often discovered in houses less than one year old. The magnitude of this defect was proved by a recent survey of a thousand homes, 10 years or older, in the New York area, which showed 59 per cent termite infestation. In some areas, the VA and the FHA require expert termite inspection and certification before approving mortgages on houses 5 years old or older.

Small, flattened mud tubes, about the size of a pencil, running along walls, and in other places connecting earth and wood, are positive signs of infestation. Termites use these tunnels as communication channels to travel between ground and wood, since termites cannot be exposed to light. Termites can also be present without tell-tale tunnels, so don't stop your inspection simply because tunnels aren't found. Probe into all accessible wooden structures with an ice pick or a thin knife blade. If the blade sinks deeply and easily into wood, it usually means interior damage, and a professional termite inspection is indicated.

Wood construction should be at least 6 inches (preferably 12 inches) above ground, with metal termite barriers around the foundation. Dead tree stumps, both above and below ground, are a natural attraction for termites, as they provide excellent breeding facilities. Scrap lumber and wood chips, buried in the ground as the lot was filled, also attract and breed termites. While these hazards might be many feet from the building, termites will eventually develop a network of tunnels to connect their breeding spots with the building.

Avoid damp houses, those that have serious cracks and openings in foundations, or are littered with scrap wood; also houses around which tunnels or positive infestation signs are found. Although the presence of termites is a serious matter, don't pass up a house solely because of this. In many cases, a few hundred dollars can correct termite damage, while proper treatment will control recurrence.

If extermination and repairs are needed, get at least two separate bids from different, accredited, contractors and exterminating companies. A composite of their estimates for repairs and extermination will be an excellent aid to determining whether the house will be a good buy. If their inspection reveals extensive damage and deep-seated infestation, it will be advisable to pass up the property.

ROOM ARRANGEMENT

Be alert for devices used to make rooms look larger, such as mirrors across one wall, contrasting paint on walls, ceilings, etc. Also, empty rooms generally look larger than do furnished ones. Take actual room measurements to avoid possible deceptive appearances.

Careful consideration should be given to the traffic pattern. The floor plan and traffic pattern must be reasonably acceptable to everyone—or your family will not be satisfied. Each family has different requirements, but some factors remain inflexible. A traffic pattern should be deemed faulty if you must walk through the living-room to get from one room to any other, except to the dining area; also, the pattern is a poor one if you can reach the kitchen only by going through another room; or if you can't reach the bathroom from any bedroom without being seen from the daytime living area. A living-room that serves as a highway for the entire house causes unnecessary work and destroys privacy. Ideally, there should be several convenient exterior doorways, with sufficient natural ventilation.

Avoid bedrooms strung in a series in which you must pass through one to reach another; and beware of a bath too near the living-room, or a living-room used as a passageway. Space for beds shouldn't be broken by doors, windows, heat units, or closets. Estimate 7 feet of unbroken wall space for a double bed.

Double-width closets are standard for most new homes; where they are not found, it is possible the builder pinched costs in construction. Calculate your storage needs against existing facilities in the prospective house. Insufficient storage makes living uncomfortable; building closets, once you have moved in, will be expensive and will sacrifice space; so check closely before making a final decision on a house.

KITCHEN AND BATH

Since it is the center of activity, the kitchen is the most important room in the house. It should be situated conveniently to living and dining areas with free access to the outdoor service area for deliveries and disposal, without interference of household traffic. The Cornell University Housing Research Center sets the minimum kitchen space at 96 sq. ft., which would be a room 12 x 8 feet. Where a wall oven or dishwasher is to be installed, proportionately larger space should be allowed. The "work area" from sink to refrigerator, to stove, should form a triangle of about 16 feet; 6 feet from center of refrigerator to center of sink; 5 feet from center of sink to front of range; and 5 feet from range to refrigerator.

Give particular attention to adequate cabinets, storage, and counter work space. Normal use requires a minimum of from 8 to 10 ft. of counter space, including cabinets underneath. There should be sufficient cabinets for storage of canned goods, utensils, and enough surplus room for storing at least a one week's supply of groceries. Mentally arrange your present kitchen furniture, making sure ample dining space remains for your entire family. If the kitchen requires remodeling to meet your needs, figure at least $750 to $1,000 for such alterations.

Bathroom tub and sink should be checked for secure seating. Where there is doubt about calking on tub, fill it with water and see if the tub pulls away from the wall under the added weight of water. If it does, the plaster and interior structure behind has probably been affected by moisture. Bear in mind that replacing old-fashioned bathroom fixtures and a shower will cost at least

$400, and is likely to run into much heavier expenditures, plus new tile for the shower which will cost at least $100. If these are indicated, add such costs to the total price of the house.

All bathrooms must have at least one window or ventilation fan to expel steam and moisture. Another point to remember is that FHA will not approve a mortgage on a home unless the main bath can be reached from every room, without walking through any other living room.

Chapter 6

DISPOSING OF YOUR OLD HOME

Two houses of the same construction and features, in the same neighborhood, can be put up for sale simultaneously, with one selling at an attractive price, while the other might never sell—or go at a greatly reduced price. The difference between the two situations lies in the preparation of the house for the sale, how it is handled during the preliminary sales stages, and the procedures used at the time of sale.

Since more of the estimated 3,000,000 families who buy or build new homes each year have older homes to unload before taking possession of the new property, disposing of the older property presents a serious problem. The inability to sell your old home can completely destroy all dreams of the new home; or it may put you into a situation where you will be paying on two homes at one time; or, a sub-standard price for a quick sale can ruin your budget and place cruel mortgage demands on the new home.

At such a time the primary objective is to make a quick sale a goal which misleads many property owners into selling at sacrifice prices. This does not necessarily have to be the case; when a house has been properly maintained, a profit can be realized, in many cases, if the older property is correctly presented and handled during negotiations.

TRADE YOUR PRESENT HOME

The real estate industry taking a cue from the automotive industry, has made it almost as easy to trade your existing home in on a new one today, as it is to trade cars. Through the "trade-in system" property owners can frequently by-pass many sales and repurchase obstacles involved in straight cash or outright sales arrangements.

There are usually three different methods available to those trading in old homes toward new ones.

THE STRAIGHT TRADE: when the builder and home buyer agree on the value of the house to be traded, and apply the cash equity as trade-in allowance toward the new home.

THE TIME LIMIT TRADE: a transaction in which the builder agrees to build or sell the prospective home owner a new home, providing the old house is sold within a stipulated period of time. Under this arrangement the builder generally gives assistance to the purchaser in attempting to sell the old home. If the customer does not sell the old house within the stipulated period of time, the deal is automatically cancelled, without obligation.

THE TRADE IN GUARANTEE: actually a combination of the straight trade and a time limit trade arrangement. Under this type deal, the builder guarantees the new home buyer that he will take the old home at an agreed price, if it is not sold within a stipulated period of time. The builder's guaranteed price usually ranges between 80 to 90 per cent of the appraised value, minus a nominal brokerage fee. The stipulated time period is flexible; however, it generally coincides with the time required to build the new home.

As with all other phases of building, buying, or financing a home, there are two sides to this method of property disposal. Each case will have individual aspects, but let's take a look at the general advantages and disadvantages likely to be encountered during an average transaction.

ADVANTAGES: The new home buyer is usually assured under such arrangements that he will at least receive the guaranteed price for his used home.

If arrangements are made directly with the builder, the usual inconvenience of having prospective buyers for the old home trouping through on inspection tours is eliminated.

With such assurance in disposing of the old home, definite plans may be made for occupancy of the new one, even before the present home has been sold.

There is ample advance time for mortgage and financing arrangements to be made for the new home, with the added guarantee that there will be no overlap period in which payments might be required on both the old and new homes.

In a case where the cash equity from the old home exceeds the minimum down payment on the new home, the buyer can receive such difference in cash, or can substantially increase the equity in the new home—which automatically lowers monthly payments.

<u>DISADVANTAGES</u>: The big disadvantage of a trade-in deal is that the appraisal of used homes by the builder or by a real estate broker is usually lower than the owner believes them to be worth. Many such deals never go beyond the appraisal stage, simply because the owner and builder cannot agree to a price compatible to both parties.

At such a time an open mind is an absolute necessity from the home owners' standpoint. Most property owners neglect to subtract for the years they have lived in the house, and expect to get back what they paid for the building, plus all they have put into it, at time of re-sale. This—unless the surrounding property has considerably increased in value—is not an equitable viewpoint. After all, when you drive a car for a few years and then trade it in, you certainly don't expect anywhere near the original price— and you have been putting extra money into the car during the period of use. Well, houses, as well as cars pile up mileage. They get behind times in styling, appliances, locations, and fixtures—which brings about a natural rate of depreciation.

If one enters into a trade-in arrangement with an open, fair mind, such dealings can be profitable and expedient short cuts to the exchange of property no longer suited for your family, for a new piece of property adapted to your needs and living requirements.

SELLING YOUR OLD HOUSE

<u>WHEN</u>: Generally, spring is the best time of year to attempt selling a house, since the first signs of good weather bring people out to look around with an eye toward buying. Particularly, if there are children in the family, people like to get settled into new homes before the fall term of school begins, and arrangements must be started in spring to make this possible. Early fall is the next best time to sell, as families who have decided to buy want to become settled before the really bad weather sets

in. Summer time is bad, since most families are occupied with vacations and various warm-weather activities. Winter is also a bad time, because most people are reluctant to subject themselves to bad weather in shopping for a house.

SETTING THE SALE PRICE: Most homeowners have an inflated idea of the value of their houses, which results in a common tendency to overprice. This is one of the biggest faults in the individual home owner's attempting to sell his own property. A professional appraiser can be employed, for about $25 to $50, who will give a fair and equitable estimate of the property value. Your bank, or a building and loan association will be happy to recommend an appraiser. It is always a good idea to add 5 to 10 per cent to the appraisal value, which will give you bargaining power to come down a little for a quick sale.

Before placing your home on the market, check the ads for homes similar to yours in total area, neighborhood, and type of construction. Balance the going market value with your original investment, add the cost of major improvements, then subtract a fair amount for the years in which you have enjoyed use of the house. This simple formula should provide you with a reasonable asking price; but keep in mind that just about every house being advertised has that 5 to 10 per cent increase to allow for dickering, so make commensurate adjustments.

In place of hiring an appraiser, you might consult your banker, or your building and loan association official, to determine the maximum mortgage they will place on your particular property. One of the strong points in your sales talk can be the financing aspect. When talking to the lending institution, determine the percentage of mortgage loan they usually make, compare that with the maximum mortgage they will advance on the property, and you will have an official appraisal without charge. If the figures emerge compatible, this can be your major sales point, with the home buyer in many cases being able to take over your old, existing mortgage, at a saving on the down payment.

The chart on the following page will give a reasonable idea of what the present-day home buyer may look for in various price ranges of homes.

SHOULD YOU USE A BROKER: Most homeowners attempting to sell an existing home do use a Realtor or real estate broker.

Value of House	Bed-Rooms	Baths	Fire-Place	Plaster Walls	Garage Car Port	Base-Ment	Interior Decorative Stonework	Area Sq. Ft.
$ 7,000 or less	2	1	no	no	no	no	no	less than 800
$ 7,000 to 9,000	3	1	no	no	no	no	no	800
$10,000 to 12,000	3	1	no	no	yes	no	no	1,000
$12,000 to 15,000	3	1	no	no	yes	no	no	1,000 or more
$15,000 to 20,000	3	1 1/2 plus	no	yes	yes	yes	no	1,200
$20,000 and more	3 or more	2 or more	yes	yes	yes	yes	yes	1,500 upward

A Realtor is a real estate broker who is a member of the National Association of Real Estate Boards. His integrity and ability have been well established before the National Board will accept him as a member. Using a reputable broker or Realtor insures you that a realistic, fair asking price will be determined, and gives you the assurance of having professional service and guidance throughout negotiations. By using an agency you also avoid the inconvenience of having unannounced prospects, since the agency will only show the house by appointment. Such an agency will also handle the necessary advertising, and will have experience in highlighting the best features of your particular house to attraction attention and a quick sale. A competent broker is also currently informed about market conditions and demands, and he usually has a list of prospective buyers who might be interested in property of your general qualification.

The average fee for a broker is 5 or 6 per cent of the total sales price, but in a case where you have made a wise selection, he is well worth the charge. You can either list your property as a "General Listing" or an "Exclusive Listing." Under a general listing, you open the house to all brokers, owing a fee only to the one who produces a sale. Should you sell the house yourself, there is no fee due anyone.

Under an exclusive listing you name one broker as your sole agent, and he is entitled to a partial commission, even though the house should be sold through another broker. This is generally the best of the two listings, since it affords more incentive to the original broker, who will probably list it with other brokers, in the hope of a quick sale. Such a listing is of particular value when you don't have time to handle prospective buyers, or when you may be moving away from the house within a short period of time. Most brokers require that the cost of advertising be charged against the sale of the house, but such charges are generally nominal.

Some brokers also try to have property owners give them what is called "the exclusive right to sell," which means that the broker is entirely in command of the property, and even if you sell the house to a friend, the broker still receives his commission. <u>This is not a recommended agreement</u>, except in special cases of emergency, such as being transferred to another city, etc.

There is also a service known as "Multiple Listing" where a group of brokers have combined their forces and each lists all the properties any of them have to sell. Under such an arrangement no matter which broker eventually sells the property, the broker who got the original listing receives part of the commission, but you still only pay the standard fee. By and large this is probably the best way of listing property, since the property is being handled by a number of reputable brokers. With a multiple listing the property owner is frequently obligated to pay a commission fee, even though he might eventually sell the property himself, so be sure to have this point cleared before signing an agreement. Specifications for multiple listings vary from one community to another, so there is no set procedure that can be outlined to cover all sections of the country—but at least ask your broker whether or not this service is available in your area.

SELLING BY YOURSELF: In some cases it might be advantageous to handle the sale by yourself, since this will effect a savings of 5 or 6 per cent of the total price that would normally be paid as commission. This type of handling is particularly desirable if you already have one or more prospective buyers or when there is no particular hurry in making the sale, or when you are sure of being able to handle financial arrangements. But even when handling the sale yourself, you should by all means have an attorney arrange legal details and the closing. If you discover you are unable to handle the sale by yourself, you can always turn it over to a broker.

PROPER ADVERTISING: One of the biggest mistakes the average person makes in attempting to sell a house is to put a crudely lettered, home-made sign on the lawn. The few dollars spent in having a professional sign made must be considered a good investment. This advertises that you have first class property to sell—and not the ramshackled building a crudely lettered sign implies. The more people you can get to look at the house, the more incentive you are supplying to prospective buyers, since they will make a quicker decision, rather than lose out to one of the many other prospects. Ads in local newspapers are excellent, but don't skimp on a few dollars; list all the best qualities of your house in the ad. Also, best results will be obtained if run in the Friday, Saturday, and Sunday papers. There are numerous opportunities, too, for free advertising. Churches, Lodges and social organizations usually have bulletin boards for such ads. Large corporations are constantly shifting personnel, and they frequently welcome listings of individual homes which they can refer to newly arrived personnel. Many drug stores and supermarkets also have bulletin boards that welcome individual property listings.

REPAIRS PRIOR TO SALE: Nothing kills a sale quicker than a house with an unkempt exterior appearance. Missing shingles, broken steps, poor paint, neglected shrubbery, scrubby lawns—all greatly detract from sales appeal. One coat of paint might add a thousand dollars to your sales price; well-kept trees should add at least a hundred dollars each to property value; and every dollar spent on lawn care and seeding will return at least ten in the final sales price.

Dripping faucets, poor interior lighting, cluttered kitchens, can all mean quick death to a potential sale. Serious wall and ceiling cracks should be repaired, and, above all, the entire house—inside and out—should present a clean appearance. Clean out the attic and basement, and be sure that closets are neat and orderly. Cluttering of these areas immediately suggests there is insufficient storage space in the house - a point sure to kill a sale.

There is, however, always the danger of over-improving. This can be done to an extent where the improvement money cannot be recovered in the final sale price. Know the value of your property, and the neighborhood, and judge the amount to be spent on improvements accordingly. If you live in a $10,000 neighborhood, you won't be able to recover your money if you create a $12,500 house. The chart below will give you some idea of values—and how losses can be avoided.

Keep pets and children well under control during showing of the house. A transaction such as buying a house is strictly for adults, and should not be interrupted by any unnecessary distraction. Keep stairways clean and clear, and avoid unpleasant cooking odors when you know a prospective buyer is planning to visit the premises.

Disposing of Your Old Home

The figures below are based on a house valued at $10,000 in a neighborhood of homes in the $10,000 bracket.

Amount of Over-Improvement	Raises Total Cost of House to:	Actual Value of House would still be	Creating a Loss to You of:
$1,000	$11,000	$10,800	$ 200
$1,500	$11,500	$11,125	$ 375
$2,000	$12,000	$11,400	$ 600
$2,500	$12,500	$11,625	$ 875
$3,000	$13,000	$11,800	$1,200
$4,000	$14,000	$12,200	$1,800
$5,000	$15,000	$12,500	$2,500

Unless it is absolutely necessary, do not decorate the interior. This sometimes runs into considerable expense, and there is no way of telling whether or not the prospective buyer will appreciate your color schemes. If you must re-decorate, use neutral colors—whites, off-whites, grays, and beiges. Many a home sale has been killed simply because the prospective buyer's wife wanted to re-decorate in a new color before moving in, and the husband felt such an expenditure was unnecessary, because the interior had just been painted.

KEEP YOUR HOUSE FURNISHED: Experience has definitely proven that a furnished house will sell about 10 times easier than one that is unfurnished. So unless you absolutely have to move, it is provident to continue living in the house until after the sale is consummated. Furnishing and rugs make rooms look better and provide the innter satisfaction to prospective buyers that their furniture will look as well as yours. And, too, an unfurnished, unoccupied house indicates that the owners are extremely anxious to sell, and offers will unquestionably be much lower than they would be for a furnished, occupied property. If there's a fireplace, and the house is being shown during chilly or cold weather, by all means have the fire cheerfully blazing. This one factor alone lends livability to a home, and can greatly influence a sale.

ANSWERING QUESTIONS: Be able to discuss construction and building values of your home intelligently. The heating system, electrical arrangement and number of circuits, utility costs, taxes, location of schools, churches, and shopping centers, the assessments, insurance rates, and local ordinances, are all questions you should be able to answer with ease. The type of insulation, depth of the foundation, whether drain tile is around the entire footing, sewage, drainage, and other public utilities— are all subjects in which the prospective buyer will be interested, so have your answers ready for him. Also, you should know the maximum mortgage that can be obtained on the property, and have a knowledgeable understanding of the approximate monthly payments and the down payment figures that will be required of the buyer to assume ownership of the property. These figures may all be had from various agencies, free, and should be made available by you or the Realtor at the time a prospect inspects your property.

DON'T USE A HARD SELL: Trying to high-pressure a prospect is perhaps one of the most fatal mistakes in selling a home. Such tactics always imply there is an urgency to dispose of the property, and the potential buyer immediately suspects something is amiss—and he concludes that a bargain price is in order. Buying a home (as has been said before) involves perhaps the largest investment people make during their lifetimes, so they wish to be able to make up their own minds.

First and foremost, be cordial with prospects but not overly friendly. Try not to monopolize the conversation. Give them ample time to ask questions, and have your answers ready. You can easily decide between those who are sincerely interested, and the idly curious. When you find a prospect who is really interested, invite him in for a cup of coffee, or for a cold drink on the patio, allowing him to get the "feel of the home." It is a good investment to have a few coloring books for children or several games on hand, to keep children amused (and out of the way) while showing their prospective buyer parents through the house. When parents are constantly keeping check on their children, they do not fully see the best points you are trying to make, and a sale may be lost because of this distraction. When people appear interested, but price seems to be the main drawback—ask them for an offer—you may find that this will come in handy, later.

FOLLOW UP PROSPECTS: At some time during the interview, obtain the name, address, and telephone number of each prospect—then follow up the lead. Few people ever buy a home the first time they look at it. On an investment of such proportion, they want to look at other property, weigh advantages and disadvantages, and to give much thought to their purchase. When sufficient interest has been displayed, it might prove beneficial to follow up the visit with a phone call in a week or two, just to let the people know your house is still available, and that they are welcome to a further look, at their convenience. There could be one or two insignificant things they did not notice—or did not understand—holding up their decision on your property. One phone call, or a return visit, may erase doubts from their minds—and close the sale. And, too, the second visit to the house is highly desirable, since by that time they are familiar with the lay-out, and have more of that "at home" feeling—which is always conducive to closing the sale.

PRICE FLEXIBILITY: It is always wise to add from 5 to 10 per cent to the sale price you would like to receive for the house. This gives you the opportunity of "making a deal" with a prospective buyer. But don't go overboard and set a price too much above current market values. Even without a mark-up, holding out for that "last dollar" might make the difference in having a quick, clean sale—or keeping the property for many months. Statistics show that most homes, reasonably priced and in good condition, sell within the first 3 to 6 months, but that the best offers are usually received on the property during the first month it is on the market. A slight concession in price on a reasonable offer, may easily make the difference in selling fast, perhaps not being able to sell at all, or, at the least, may result in your being saddled with the property for many months—and even then taking a reduced offer.

LEGAL ASSISTANCE: The buying or selling of any property presents many potential legal booby traps, and, whether you are buying or selling, you must have an experienced lawyer represent you during all phases of the transaction. While his fee may be a hundred dollars, what may be routine handling on his part may prevent a loss of thousands of dollars to you, either in immediate outlay or savings, or in subsequent discoveries. Your lawyer will be responsible for drawing up all contracts and for determining what is to be considered "part of the house" and what might be charged extra as appliances and added improvements. The refrigerator, blinds, rugs, etc. could return to you the few extra hundred dollars you sacrificed for a quick sale, but, without legal assistance, you might be talked into including these along with the building. The prospective buyer will most certainly have an attorney - <u>which makes you extremely vulnerable without equal legal assistance</u>. In most cases the charge for legal fees are more than repaid in savings, and, in all cases, the peace of mind in knowing the deal is clear, legal and final is certainly worth such a small fee.

Chapter 7

WHAT YOU SHOULD KNOW ABOUT FINANCING AND MORTGAGES

For most homeowners, taking possession of their new homes is the happiest moment of their lives. For many others, this joyous occasion is later marked in memory by regret and financial hardship. The difference between satisfaction and regret is that some people are blinded by the excitement and don't fully realize what they are doing at the time of purchase, negotiation, and settlement. For instance, since more than 95 per cent of all homes, built or bought, are financed with mortgages, there are some things you must know to prevent catastrophe overtaking you when you acquire your new home.

Consider the ant—one of Nature's most responsible builders. He is a hard, energetic worker, but, more important, he knows that he can carry on his back fifteen times—and no more than fifteen times—his own weight. Before you contract for a mortgage, consider the <u>total price</u> of everything connected with the new home. The financial weight which <u>you can carry safely</u> is your most important consideration. Your failure to take a close look at your financial strength could make the mortgage a burden of crushing responsibility.

Experienced mortgage institutions usually answer this problem with an unwritten rule that the <u>total cost</u> of the home should not exceed two-and-a-half times your yearly <u>take home pay</u>. So, if you have a <u>net</u> paycheck of $10,000 you may safely plan on buying a home not to exceed $25,000, all costs included. Seasoned investors further break this down to another rule-of-thumb, that the monthly payments (including principle, interest, taxes, insurance, etc.) should not exceed your weekly <u>net</u> income, while the more cautious money lenders go one step further, and say that such monthly payments should include cost of heating and other utilities, and <u>still</u> not exceed the weekly net income.

One serious—often disastrous—mistake made at this point, especially with young married couples, is to count on the wife's income. Since nature continues to dominate the actions of mankind, the usual result is that within a year ot wo the couple find themselves blessed with an offspring and the wife is busy tending to his or her needs. This not only eliminates the wife's income, but inevitably adds expense, so, the entire program is seriously upset.

Another thought to consider is the monthly pay, in terms of what might lie ahead, instead of today's income. Presently your income might justify $125 monthly payments, but, if you have reached your salary peak, or plan to enlarge the family, then some serious thought should be given to the total amount of monthly payment you may be able to absorb safely a few years from today. While your salary may remain the same, the household expenses will undoubtedly increase in proportion to the increase in your family.

<u>SHOPPING FOR THE MORTGAGE</u>: The bank officials where you have your account, or the insurance company with whom you have been carrying insurance, or the credit union where you work, are all good places to start your mortgage shopping. Many banks and insurance companies restrict their investments to certain neighborhoods, but, if this is the case, they will refer you to some other reliable institution that will handle your specific needs.

Regardless of where you go, don't take the first offer. A lending institution (or individual) survives only as long as they can continue to invest money. Therefore, you will find almost as many variations in terms and interest rates as between competitive supermarkets. Get at least <u>three</u> estimates on your particular needs before you make the final decision. Ask about interest rates, terms, settlement costs and restrictive terms of the contract, and make notes of these for comparison with other offers.

Ask the lending institution these questions:

1. How long will it take for the loan to go through?

2. What is the interest rate; and what will the <u>total interest</u> be over the life of the mortgage?
3. How large will the monthly payments be, and for how many years?
4. Do payments include taxes, water, insurance, etc., or what extra costs will you be called upon to pay, in addition to the regular mortgage payments?
5. In what manner are payments to be made, and is there a period of grace for lateness?
6. Exactly what will your insurance cover?
7. Can the mortgage be paid off in advance, without penalty, and will this be written into the contract?
8. What coverage do you get from the title insurance?

QUESTIONS THE LENDING INSTITUTION WILL ASK YOU:

1. What are your current debts and bills. (Have this ready and broken down into automobile, furniture, clothing, etc.)
2. What life insurance do you carry?
   (Life and medical, automobile, etc., should be listed)
3. What is your monthly take-home pay. (They will also want to know the gross, but are more concerned with take-home pay.)
4. They will probably ask for a copy of your last year's income tax return.
5. What family obligations do you have? (This includes children in school, support of parents, relatives, etc.)
6. A list of your credit references.
7. At least three personal references.
8. What are your current monthly expenses. (Have this broken down into utilities, household expense, food, clothing, entertainment, current bills, etc.)

LENGTH OF MORTGAGE: A mortgage is a debt secured by your home and land. It is a regular monthly expense that must be met, so the sooner you can get it paid, the more money you will have for other living expenses. In setting up the mortgage payment plan, select the shortest term policy you can <u>comfortably handle</u>. While a five-year plan may not fit your income bracket a twenty-five-year plan may not be the answer, either.

Somewhere in between you may find a compatible program that can be worked into your budget without financial hardship—and without dragging the payments out any longer than necessary.

The longer the mortgage runs, the more money you are paying in interest. For instance, if you borrow $10,000 for 5 years, at 5 per cent interest, you will pay $1,323.20 in interest during that time. For the same $10,000, spread over a 25-year plan, you will be paying a total of $7,538 interest. This amounts to a difference of $6,214.80, or better than 60 per cent of the entire face value of the loan. And don't think that interest rates aren't important. While a half per cent might seem insignificant, it can amount to a lot of money over a span of years. See the chart for the difference between a 5 per cent and a 5-1/2 per cent loan. That 1/2 of 1 per cent difference costs an additional $885 on $10,000 for 25 years.

Monthly payments required to amortize a loan in the number of years and for amounts shown. (Payments may vary slightly with different institutions and tax problems, and will probably be a trifle higher for interest in west coast areas.)

Interest	Amount	10 years	15 years	20 years	25 years
5%	5,000	53.04	39.54	33.00	29.23
	10,000	106.07	79.08	66.00	58.46
	15,000	159.10	118.62	99.00	87.69
	20,000	212.14	158.16	132.00	116.92
5-1/4%	5,000	53.65	40.20	33.70	29.97
	10,000	107.30	80.39	67.39	59.93
	15,000	160.94	120.59	101.08	89.89
	20,000	214.59	160.78	134.77	119.85
6%	5,000	55.52	42.20	35.83	32.22
	10,000	111.03	84.39	71.65	64.44
	15,000	166.54	126.58	107.47	96.65
	20,000	222.05	168.78	143.29	128.87
6-1/2%	5,000	56.78	43.56	37.28	33.77
	10,000	113.55	87.12	74.56	67.53
	15,000	170.33	130.67	111.84	101.29
	20,000	227.10	174.23	149.12	135.05

What You Should Know About Financing and Mortgages

Generally, V. A. loans carry the lowest interest rates, with FHA loans next, and the conventional mortgages carrying the highest rate. However, conventional institutions may go as low as 5 per cent on large amounts, or where the loan is heavily secured.

Total Cost of Interest for a $10,000 Mortgage

Interest Rate	Years of Mortgage	Monthly Payments	Total Interest Paid
5%	5 yrs.	188.72	$1,323.20
	10 yrs.	106.07	2,728.40
	15 yrs.	79.08	4,234.40
	20 yrs.	66.00	5,840.00
	25 yrs.	58.46	7,538.00
5-1/2%	5 yrs.	191.02	$1,461.20
	10 yrs.	108.53	3,023.60
	15 yrs.	81.71	4,707.80
	20 yrs.	68.79	6,509.60
	25 yrs.	61.41	8,423.00

OPEN END MORTGAGE: Naturally, we all anticipate advancement in our respective fields, which will bring about additional income. Humans, being optimistic by nature, are all prone to making plans on this potentiality. For such an event, and other sound reasons, it is always advisable to obtain what is known as an "open end mortgage." Under such a contract, should your dreams come true, you can pay off the mortgage far in advance of the term specified, with little or no penalty. Without such provisions made in advance, some institutions will charge extremely stiff penalties for advance payments.

But make sure this pre-payment feature is written into the mortgage contract. By the same token, should your dreams not materialize, and you need money in later years for improvements, additional rooms, or modern utilities and appliances, you can obtain such needed financing under the same contract. This is particularly desirable when, at the time of purchase, the budget doesn't allow all the space or facilities that might be later required. When the time comes to add such improvements, the funds are available under long-term, low interest rates—as compared to short term and high interest that would probably otherwise be demanded. This consolidates all payments in one package, instead of necessitating regular monthly payments to two different accounts. It also saves you refinancing and other costs, but sometimes a charge is made for a new title search. This kind of additional loan can be included in your present mortgage, either by increasing the monthly payments, or by extending the mortgage, to absorb the additional money. Either way, you are better off with this type of contract.

TYPES OF MORTGAGES: Basically there are three general categories of mortgages: the conventional; the VA-guaranteed; the F.H.A. insured. Differences in circumstances and individuals make these three varied types of loans both necessary and desirable. Almost all mortages of today are self amortizing, which means the principle and interest are paid off by specified monthly payments, throughout the life of the mortgage contract.
On most mortgages, the monthly payment remains the same for the life of the contract, with a progressively larger sum being applied to the principle each month, as the total loan amount decreases. In effect, this means that while you continue to pay the same amount, more of the payment is being applied to the original loan and a little less to the interest, since the lender only draws interest from the actual balance.

CONVENTIONAL MORTGAGE: The terms of a conventional mortgage are usually worked out on an individual basis between you and the lender. Most conventional lenders, whether individuals or institutions, ask for a one-third down payment, which is called the "initial equity." In cases where you are building, and own the ground free and clear, the price of the land is generally included as part of the down payment, since the mortgage will cover the land as well as the house. Banks, which usually appraise at 10 per cent below sales value, will normally go up to 65 per cent of the wholesale price, which roughly figures out to about 1/2 the retail value. Savings and Loan Associations work from

What You Should Know About Financing and Mortgages

the retail price, and normally go up to 65 per cent of that figure. Such loans will probably take about 10 days for completion.

According to figures recently released by the National Association of Real Estate Boards, conventional mortgages have a prevailing interest rate of 6 per cent in half the country, and 6-1/4 to 6-1/2 per cent in the other areas. On large amounts, or heavily secured loans, it is possible to find 5 per cent mortgages in many cases.

VA GUARANTEED MORTGAGES: Under a VA-guaranteed mortgage, veterans may secure loans guaranteed through the Veterans Administration. Because of this guarantee, it is possible to obtain a loan with very little or, in many cases, no down payment. They will guarantee up to 60 per cent of a loan, or $7,500, whichever amount is less. On large mortgages, this can frequently be worked out with a combination VA and FHA deal to cover the excess balance. Because of the low interest rate (5-1/4 per cent) most institutions are reluctant to make this type of loan, since they can get higher rates on other contracts.

On this type of loan the property is inspected by federal inspectors before their stamp of approval is given. If the price is out of reason, or if the house is not constructed according to government specifications, they will either demand adjustment, or disapprove the application. Because of this inspection, and the necessary government paper work, this type of loan takes at least 5 weeks to be completed.

FHA INSURED MORTGAGE: Under this type loan, the government, through the Federal Housing Administration, insures the lender against loss in case of default by the borrower. With such a guarantee, lending institutions generally accept a smaller down payment than under a conventional loan. Under the new FHA law 87-70 of 1961, down payments under FHA mortgages are 3 per cent up to $15,000, 10 per cent from $15,000 to $20,000, and 25 per cent from $20,000 upwards. They will insure mortgages up to $25,000 on one-family homes; $27,500 on two- or three-family homes; $35,000 on four-family homes. Down payment includes all closing costs, and mortgages have a high ceiling of a maximum of 6 per cent, with many lending institutions giving mortgages of 5-1/4, 5-1/2 and 5-3/4 per cent under insured FHA loans. Maximum term of insurance of FHA loans are 35 years for new homes, 30 years for existing homes—with extensions of time up to 40 years being allowed in cases of families displaced because of slum clearance, etc. This type of loan usually takes at least 5 weeks for completion. Again, government appraisers examine the property, and the price and condition of the home must meet with their specifications before the loan is approved. Provisions can also be made under this type of loan for acquiring household appliances, under a "package" program.

CONSTRUCTION LOANS: Banks and other lending institutions have special arrangements for building projects—called construction loans. They make arrangements to pay for materials and labor as the home is being built, then, upon its completion, they switch over to a permanent mortgage for the balance.

Payments will be made in stages, with interest being charged only for the money actually given you. Interest rates for this type of loan are usually 1/2 of 1 per cent per month, for actual amounts of cash which they supply. They will, for instance, supply a small operating capital; and the next advance will probably come when the foundation is installed; followed by advances upon completion of the roof, installation of rough utilities, etc., until the building is ready for occupancy. They will work out a regular schedule with you, so that necessary money will always be available. One of the good features of this type of loan is that their representatives will make regular inspections of the construction. This not only protects their investment, but gives you a double check on work quality and progress.

HIDDEN COSTS: In figuring the total cost of buying or building a new home, many little factors must be considered. If these hidden costs are overlooked, the ultimate figure can add up so heavily, it can wreck your entire program. First there is the possibility of special assessments, so inquire carefully into this. Then, consider whether the land will require grading, landscaping, a possible driveway, or other necessary improvements.

Again, on existing houses—will storm doors and windows be needed—and, if so, how much will they cost? What about utilities and appliances? Many times these items may be incorporated into the mortgage, if they are considered before the contract is signed. Then there will be garden tools, power equipment, or other items that cost money.

Or perhaps an appraisal fee will be necessary on a conventional mortgage, which will cost about $75; or a survey will be needed to determine exact boundaries of the property line, which will run another $50 to $75; the title search, recording fees, attorney fees; all are costly and must be considered for a true picture of how much it will cost to move into your new home. Discuss all these potential expenses with your attorney and the lender, and be sure you can handle the immediate outlay of cash without completely wiping out your savings. You will need still more money for moving expenses and for the many little things that will be necessary once you take up occupancy. And don't forget that your maintenance and expense, which will continue to accumulate, can be figured at approximately 12 per cent of the total cost of the house.

ABSTRACT: An abstract is a complete record of a particular piece of property, going back to the time the title resided in the government, and up to the present. Throughout the years, registered "abstract companies," have specialized in this kind of record search. Their attorneys carefully check all records and render complete, accurate, concise statements of the pertinent, legally significant facts appearing on the public records. A complete tax search, certified as to correctness, is made of the property abstracted.

TITLE INSURANCE: When mortgages are protected by title insurance their marketability is enhanced and they can be assigned more quickly. Almost all lending institutions will require this before they grant the loan. In issuing a title insurance policy, the abstract company contracts to indemnify the insured against any loss that may be suffered by reason of any claims, defects, encumbrances, or marketability of the title. Should something untoward arise, the company will defend the title and bear all the costs of litigation. Only one premium is required on such a policy—the one payable at the time of issue. The most prominent types of title policies are: the "owner's"—which protects one having owner's interest; and the "mortgage" policy—which protects the lender.

Title insurance rates, for ordinary risks, based upon a single chain of title when the applicant submits a satisfactory abstract, are about $35 for the first one thousand dollars of liability, and approximately $5 for each additional thousand dollars. This means that on a $10,000 home, the title insurance rate would be about $80. If there are unusual problems attending your application or property, or if other special services are required, the company may make small additional charges, commensurate to the worth of such added service.

LEGAL ADVICE: Although the services of an attorney will add approximately another hundred dollars to the settlement costs, when this is compared to the amount being invested, the fee is entirely reasonable. Legal assistance is definitely recommended in buying or in settling property, and can prove much more valuable than you might ever imagine. Have an attorney from the very beginning, so he may supervise every step of the proceedings. It is often very difficult—and sometimes impossible —for an attorney to unravel things *after* you discover that someone has blundered, or that an intentional error has been made. In the interpretation of the policy and contracts, many matters arise which require professional services. Even if you do read the many clauses in fine print yourself, you probably won't understand exactly what is designated—or implied. If you are building your own home, legal services are even more important for drawing up the various contracts and agreements and for keeping a trained eye on the many transactions.

SERVICES AN ATTORNEY PERFORMS:

1. Checks for existing mortgages if sale is part cash, with the balance through assumption of an existing mortgage.
2. Checks accrued and unpaid interest you assume on existing mortgages.
3. Determines that all taxes are paid by the seller for past years, and his proportionate part of taxes for the current year, up to date of sale.

What You Should Know About Financing and Mortgages

4. Determines whether or not water bills have been paid to date.
5. Secures proper receipts for release fees and recording charges.
6. Insures that the revenue stamps on the deed are in proper order, for buyers frequently inadvertently pay for such stamps, not knowing their rights.
7. Checks the abstract or title insurance commitment.

YOUR ATTORNEY WILL ALSO SECURE

1. A legal and properly executed deed.
2. Proper abstract or title policy.
3. Bills of sale covering possible personal property involved in the transaction, such as rugs, drapes, appliances, etc.
4. Duly signed receipts for money paid into purchase price.
5. Statement from the lending institution showing the full amount due on the loan, so later claims cannot be made that a greater amount is due.
6. Proper fire and casualty insurance policies that adequately cover the costs and needs for your protection as well, as the lending agency.
7. Up to date receipts on taxes, special assessments, and other municipal obligations.

INSURANCE: The individual lender, or institution, will automatically include sufficient hazard insurance in the monthly payments to protect his or their investment. Check this carefully, since often your equity is not adequately covered under the same policy. For instance, if a bank lends you $10,000 and you have $5,000 cash in the property, there are many cases in which only the mortgage value is covered. The difference in cost between the two amounts for complete coverage is relatively small, and you certainly want to protect your investment, as well as that of the lending institution. At the same time, make sure the policy includes the "extended coverage" clause, which will reimburse you for damages by explosion, wind, hail, aircraft, etc.

There is also an insurance plan available through several companies, whereby, for an additional one per cent of the annual payment, you can guarantee ownership of your home to your heirs. This is called "mortgage redemption" insurance, which consists of a combination of Ordinary Life insurance and term coverage. In effect, this plan may be worked out in such a way that, should you meet with an untimely death prior to completion of the mortgage, you family would receive a free and clear title, plus a little cash, with which to continue their standard of living. Or, should you survive the terms of your mortgage contract, there will be sufficient cash value accrued on the Ordinary Life part of the policy, to enable you to pay off the mortgage several years in advance of the normal mortgage span. Either way, this makes a good addition to any mortgage, and is worth investigating.

Chapter 8

TRICKS IN SAVING MONEY WHEN BUILDING

Anyone contemplating building a new home can actually save a minimum of 25 per cent of the total cost. While this might seem an overstatement, it is possible and this savings is available to anyone who has the desire for a home, plus a little knowledge of business coordination. You don't have to be a handyman-craftsman. In fact, you won't be required to drive a single nail. Your savings will largely be realized through absorbing the expensive administrative and purchasing profits normally associated with construction work.

This is the type of project on which a husband and wife can work together. Getting the program started in the only big problem, and this diminishes each time you contact a new source of information and assistance. Once the program is formulated, the combined efforts of husband and wife can carry it through to a successful conclusion, with Hubby still being able to put in full-time on his job.

Admittedly, this is a more difficult way to acquire a home than just turning the entire problem over to an architect and a contractor. True, such paid professional men will do an admirable job — for equally admirable fees — and you will have a sturdy home; but, you can actually have fun building your own home. It will be just as sturdy, and when it is finished, you will not only realize a savings of at least 25 per cent, but the finished product will represent more than a mass of lumber and masonry; it will be something you have built yourself. Whatever headaches you may encounter with building problems will all be repaid on the day you walk into your new home.

(<u>See</u>: Building Cost Breakdown Chart)

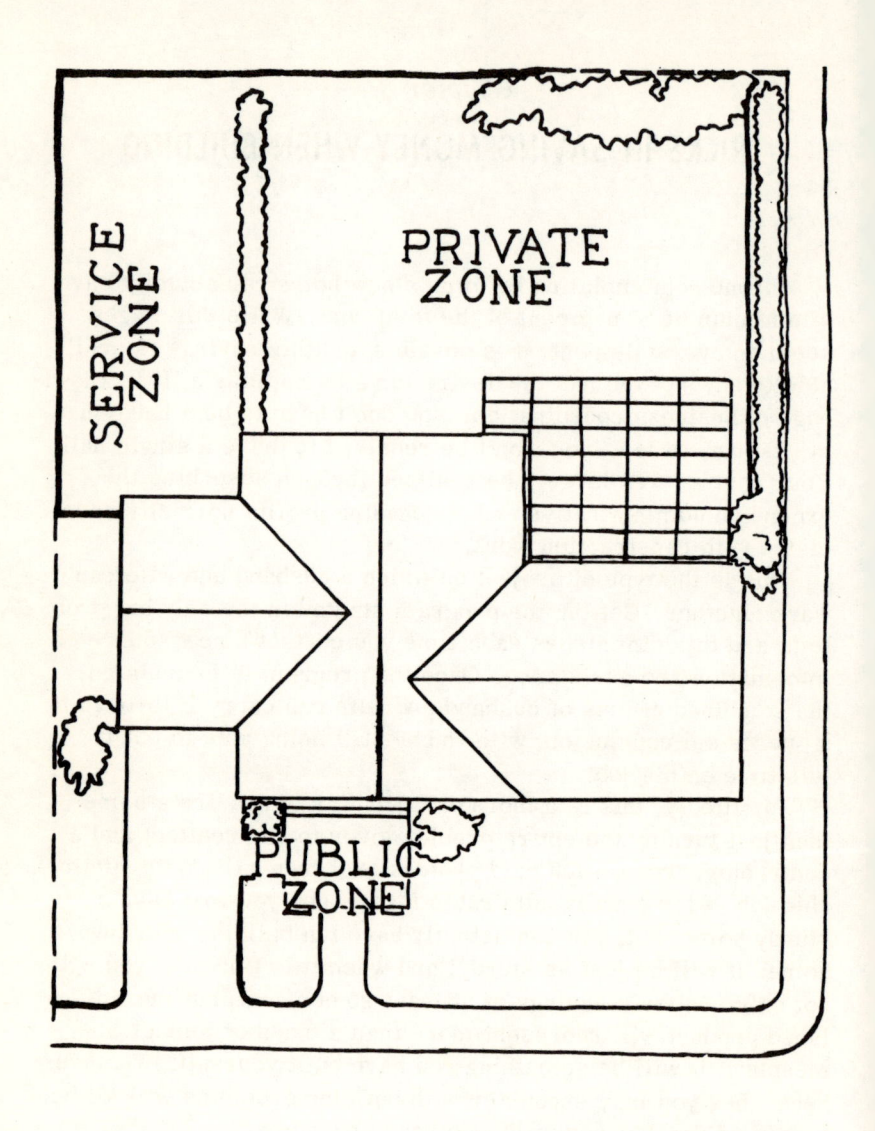

With this particular zoning lay-out, the house faces the rear of the lot to provide maximum use of a small site, and to give a large private zone.

Tricks in Saving Money When Building

ARCHITECT: An architect will charge a standard minimum fee of 5 per cent of the total home value, which amounts to $1,250.00 for a $25,000 home. This entire amount can be saved!

Several magazines and plan-books feature drawings, specifications, and materials lists for modern homes, which have been created and prepared by registered, nationally recognized architects. You have your choice of several dozen different designs and types of homes — with prints, specifications and lists of materials — available for from $10.00 to $35.00, depending upon the source. For this nominal charge you will receive the same information and drawings you'd get from an individual architect for the 5 or 10 per cent fee.

Of course, you won't have the latitude of personal changes in building design that you would normally have through a private architect, but, among the many types and models offered by this package plan, you'll almost certainly find at least one plan that will just about meet your every requirement. The few little things that might be missing may be substituted as you go along. And, let's face it, for a lump savings of at least $1,215.00 (the minimum $1,250 fee minus $35 for plans) you can probably get along without a few little personal innovations.

GENERAL CONTRACTOR: General contractors earn their living building homes for other people, usually charging 5 per cent of the total cost as overhead, plus another 10 per cent fee as profit for handling the job. On a $25,000 home, where $20,000 is spent on materials and construction, the general contractor charges can run up to $3,000 — as shown in items 18 and 19 of the Building Cost Breakdown Chart. This is $3,000 you can save by handling the general contracting yourself!

Negotiating for materials and labor is not as difficult as it might seem. With only a nodding acquaintance of what goes into a home, and a basic idea of how it is built, you can do your own contracting. Primarily, in addition to supplying material and arranging for various workmen to perform the specific stages of building, the biggest part of contracting is coordination and timing. Knowing when to have which craftsmen ready for specific phases of work, plus having them and materials at the building site when needed — is the basic function of contracting.

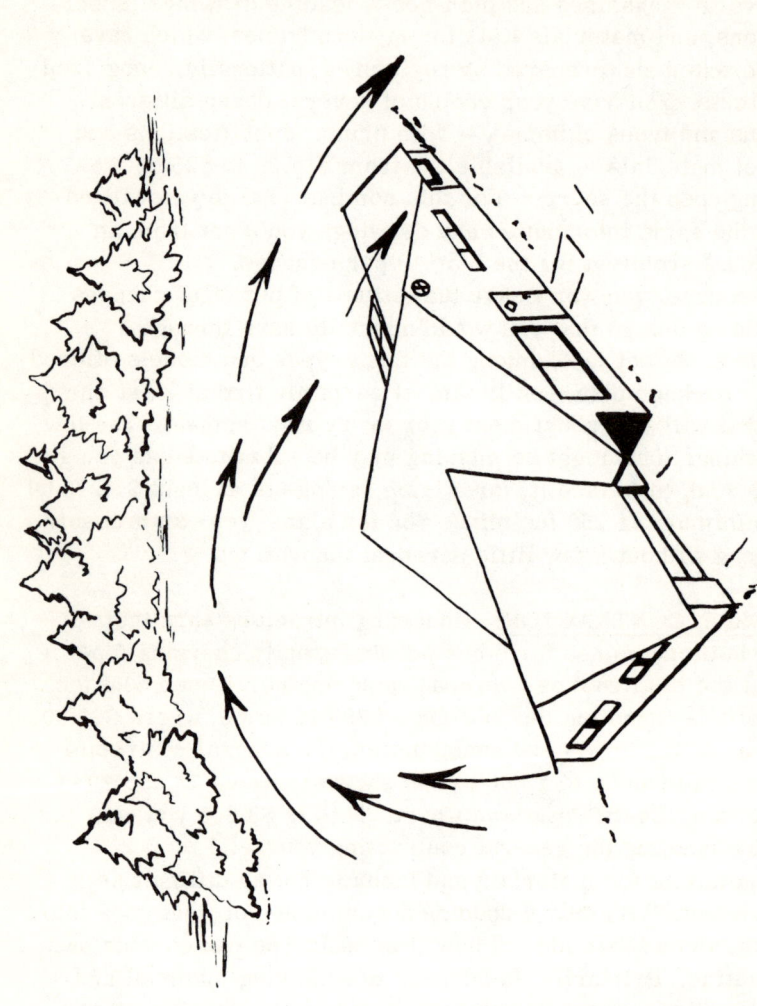

Curving evergreen hedges to the north and east trap cool summer breezes and will also serve as an effective windbreak and snow fence during winter months.

Tricks in Saving Money When Building

You are going to be at the building location as much as possible anyway, so why not do your own coordination and save the 15 per cent?

In addition to the $3,000 saved through handling your own contracting, you will also save appreciable amounts in discounts on the numerous bulk purchases. When a contractor handles a building project, you pay standard market values, with discounts in most cases going to the contractor doing the actual purchasing.

SUB-CONTRACTING: Under the usual method of home building, the general contractor engages a sub-contractor to hire skilled workers and to carry out specific phases of the construction. For this service, the subcontractor generally charges a flat 5 per cent for overhead, plus another 5 or 10 per cent for profit on what he handles. For instance, the subcontractor for concrete and masonry would take at least $160 and possibly $240 of the total amount allocated for this phase of work, as his overhead and profit. Normally, he personnally doesn't do any of the actual work, but merely guarantees that men will be at the building site to do the work when needed. His fee also includes inspection of the work during construction and when the job is finished.

You can make arrangements for skilled craftsmen to be on hand when needed; and you can also arrange for municipal building inspectors to give the work a _free_ professional inspection, which adds another substantial savings.

Extend this same overhead plus profit percentage over the entire job; carpentry, plumbing, electrical work, etc. A considerable portion of your building fund can be saved through personally handling liaison work with various craftsmen. You can effect at least a $1,500.00 saving by making individual arrangements with the workers.

An attorney will be necessary for buying the land, making financial arrangements, settling the mortgage, so have him draw up suitable contracts for the various work groups you will be hiring. The public utility companies will supply free inspection of electrical, gas, water, and heating installation; municipal building inspectors, plus routine inspections from your money lending agency, will cover the other phases of construction, guaranteeing that terms of good workmanship in your contract have been satisfactorily met.

How do you find the various skilled workers you'll need? There are several ways. Friends and neighbors who have had work done by individual craftsmen can recommend many sources to you. By careful selection, you can get the various stages of work done quicker and cheaper — and a better job. By analogy — if you have trouble with your eyes, you go to see an eye specialist — not a general doctor. The same applies to building. Carpentry, for instance, has many specialty fields. Some carpenters specialize in laying hardwood flooring, some in building stairs, finishing attics, installing windows, etc. These men will do a better job in less time than a general hammer and nail wood worker. Because the work is done faster, cost is automatically saved through less labor hours; and, because the men are skilled in that particular field, material is saved.

Various union halls, the Yellow Pages of your telephone directory, stopping at various places where building is being done, and talking with the workers — are all good sources for the location of skilled labor for your building. Your lumber dealer, building supply operator, or any other dealer supplying material for your home, will all know competent men in that particular field of construction, with whom they have been dealing for years, and whose work and reputation they can vouch for.

Whenever possible, hire out each building phase by the completed job — not on an hourly or daily wage basis. In that way you won't have to stand over the workers every minute, to protect your hourly dollar rate. Any loafing they do will be on their own time — so, little if any delay will be experienced — and no money will come out of your pocket if something slows the workers down. When common labor is needed to conserve skilled hours — such as a mortar mixer and hod carrier for a brick mason — have this figured into the one package price from the beginning. It would be foolish, and costly, to have a professional mason mixing and carrying his own mortar, at $4.00 an hour or more, when a common laborer could do such work for $2.00 an hour or less.

Have your building schedule not only arranged well in advance, but flexible enough to allow a day or so between each separate

Tricks in Saving Money When Building 89

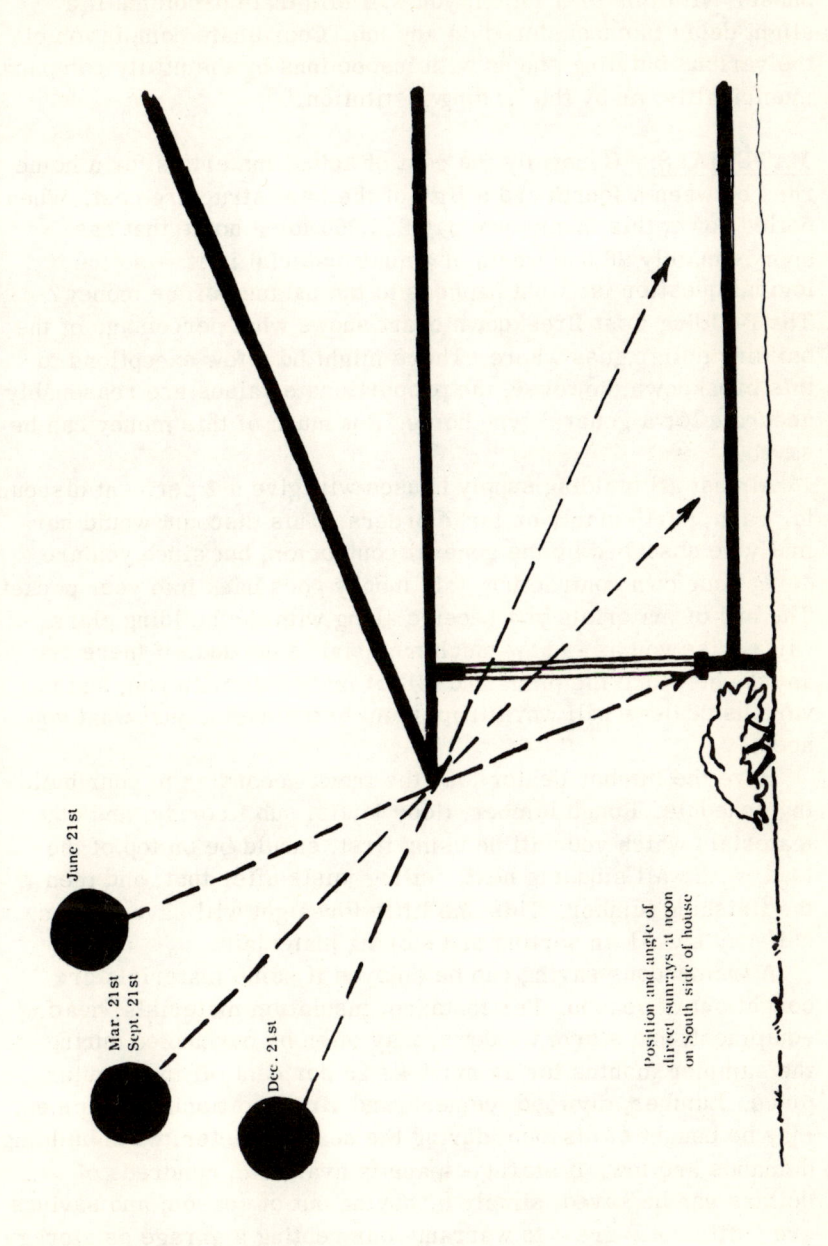

June 21st

Mar. 21st
Sept. 21st

Dec. 21st

Position and angle of
direct sunrays at noon
on South side of house

phase. With this precaution, you will eliminate problems if a slight delay is encountered on any job. Coordinate completion of the various building stages with inspections by the utility company, municipality, or by the lending institution.

MATERIALS: Generally the cost of actual materials for a home runs between a fourth and a fifth of the total structure cost. When boiled down, this means you pay $25,000 for a home that has approximately $6,000 worth of actual material in it — so the logical question is: what happens to the balance of the money? The Building Cost Breakdown chart shows what percentage of the building dollar goes where. There might be a few exceptions to this breakdown; however, the proportionate values are reasonably accurate for a general type home. But much of this money can be saved.

Almost all building supply houses will give a 2 per cent discount for cash, particularly on large orders. This discount would normally be absorbed by the general contractor, but since you are doing your own contracting, this money goes back into your pocket. The bill of materials you receive along with the building plans will advise you as to how much material is needed. If there are any doubts, take the plans and bill of materials with you, and the various dealers will work from them to determine just what you need.

Have the lumber dealer load the truck according to your building schedule. Rough lumber, floor joists, sub flooring, and other materials which you will be using first, should be on top of the load, with wall studding next, ceiling joists after that, and then the finishing lumber. This one little foresight will save about a half-day's work in sorting and storing materials.

A tremendous saving can be enjoyed if some materials are bought out of season. For instance, insulation materials, heating equipment, and storm windows, may often be purchased during the summer months for as much as 25 per cent off the regular price. Lumber, plywood, cement, and air-conditioning equipment may be bought at discount during the dead of winter, when building demands are low. If storage space is available, hundreds of dollars can be saved, simply by buying out of season; and savings are sufficiently great to warrant your renting a garage as storage

Tricks in Saving Money When Building 91

space, since the few dollars spent in monthly rent will be more than repaid by savings enjoyed.

Since labor cost is the biggest part of your construction bill, buy materials with the thought of saving labor as well as money. Plywood and hardboard panels, for example, will save many hours of labor at $3.00 and better an hour. By using plywood panels, exterior walls, roof sheathing and sub-flooring can be installed in only a fraction of the time normally required for the same job with 6-inch boards. In this manner great savings can be effected in labor costs, without sacrifice to quality.

Where wall-to-wall carpeting is to be used, the expense of finished flooring may be skipped, with 3/4-inch plywood used as subflooring. You will save enough money from omitting the finished flooring, to almost pay for the carpeting.

ELECTRICAL: If your electric power company provides free lay-out and planning service (and most of them do), you will receive considerable benefit from this service. (See: Free Service Chart). Engineers provided by utility companies are paid fixed salaries, and they receive no commission for sales resulting from their suggestions. Since they have no personal gain, you may safely assume their advice is given solely to your best interest. They will suggest fixtures, materials and arrangements to provide for best living at a minimum cost. Independent lighting engineers would charge several hundred dollars for this same service, provided free by power companies.

Utility companies will often arrange for inspection during construction, of wiring, entrance box and other electrical components. In places where electric companies don't provide such service, municipal inspectors, and qualified examiners from the lending institution, are available to make construction inspections for safety and adequacy of electric installations. In sections where utility companies do not sell the actual appliances and materials themselves they will be happy to recommend an accredited dealer. Discounts are seldom offered by power companies, but most dealers will provide discounts for cash.

The dealer will gladly supply names of several licensed electricians for installation of wiring, etc. Talk to at least two of them for price, time element, etc., before making your final choice.

Summer Sunset 7:30 P.M.

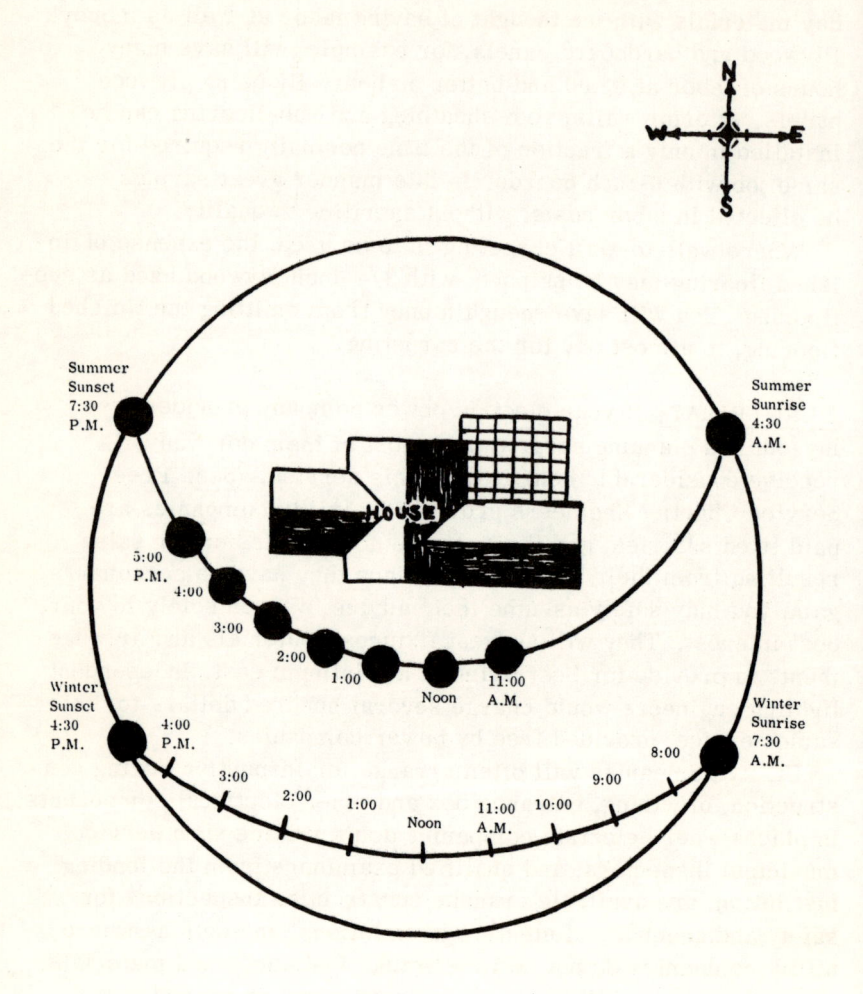

Summer Sunrise 4:30 A.M.

5:00 P.M.
4:00
3:00
2:00
1:00
Noon
11:00 A.M.

Winter Sunset 4:30 P.M.
4:00 P.M.
3:00
2:00
1:00
Noon
11:00 A.M.
10:00
9:00
8:00

Winter Sunrise 7:30 A.M.

Tricks in Saving Money When Building

Electric ranges, washers, hot water heaters, and heating systems, are often installed free of charge by many electric power companies. This, itself, can result in sizeable savings to you, so, don't overlook this possibility.

PLUMBING: The plumbing supply houses from whom you purchase pipes and fixtures will unquestionably put you into contact with licensed, reputable plumbers to carry out installation.

Since, at this point, you have probably already talked to the municipal plumbing inspectors, you have a good idea of the essential requirements of your locality. The supply house of representatives will fill you in on accessories. Talk to the plumbers well in advance of starting construction, determining the total cost of their work — how long it will take, and how much advance notice will be required for them to be ready for work at a given time.

Installation of pipe must be coordinated with roughing-in of the house, while drains will probably have to be coordinated with setting the foundation. Determine these particulars and set your schedule accordingly. Don't overlook the fact that plumbing supply houses operate on at least a 2 per cent discount for cash, which can figure out to a tidy sum on this large expenditure.

Get estimates from at least two supply houses and plumbers before making a final decision on either phase. You might find that prices, for identical material or labor, will vary appreciably. If you are going to include an automatic washer in your appliance program, the dealer might allow an additional discount to cover part of the installation cost, as your subcontracted plumbers will be doing all the work.

HEATING: Investigate different types of heating plants before making the final decision. Oil, electric, and gas heat all have specific advantages. Talk to friends who have these various heating plants, and learn from them their experience as to both advantages and disadvantages, plus operating costs, since these will be a big factor in the years ahead. The least expensive plant to install is not necessarily the best dollar value — when years of heating costs are considered.

Factory representatives of different oil burner companies will supply pertinent costs, in some cases making the installation free. They will also recommend licnesed mechanics who have worked with them over the years and have proved to be reliable. Again, don't forget to inquire about a discount for cash.

Electric or gas heat will probably be handled through the local utility company, with their engineers and technicians giving you full details on capacity, cost, and operation. Most utility companies will install their heating plants free, others will make installation at an absolute minimum charge. Get a complete set of figures on all heating systems; then balance costs, advantages, and disadvantages, before making your selection.

Don't overlook the fact that the 1961 Housing Act allows FHA to insure loans on experimental heating units. Maybe your new home will be geographically adapted to solar heat — or to some other innovation that you may wish to try.

AIR CONDITIONING: Check with the Free Service Chart to determine whether or not your utility company provides planning and lay-out for air conditioning. They will advise you as to the best location of units and the proper size of conditioners for given areas, and they will also provide a complete air-conditioning plan for one section, or for the entire house — whichever you desire. This professional service alone might save hundreds of dollars through efficient location and proper selection of units, plus overall operation costs through the years to come. Why pay more in basic cost and operation for a 1-ton unit, when a 3/4-ton would service just as efficiently? Such an unnecessary cost will be eliminated by obtaining this professional service.

Utility companies who plan and lay-out either heating or air conditioning will also provide complete information and advice on insulation. A certain type of insulation might have worked wonderfully well on Cousin Pete's home, but this doesn't mean that the same material will be good for you. A poor selection of insulation will cost you many dollars, over the years, in heating and air conditioning. So professional advice on this phase of building is important.

It is advisable to have definite heating and air conditioning plans formulated early in your program. Once this problem is settled, you can deal more intelligently with the insulation and other building factors. Therefore, even if you plan to install air conditioning later, make plans in your building for it now.

Tricks in Saving Money When Building

OTHER CONSTRUCTION: Plastering and lathing is an expensive, important part of home building, and it should be done by experienced men. Considerable savings may be effected in this phase of building by using sheets of hardboard, or wallboard in some areas, instead of plaster. A wall can be efficiently finished, with large sheets of hardboard or wallboard, in a fraction of the time it would require highly priced plasterers to do the same area. Discuss this situation with the building supply dealer, municipal building inspectors, and engineers from whom you get your heating and air conditioning advice. Depending upon the type of home — and the use designated for the various rooms — substantial savings in labor costs may be possible by using large sheets, rather than having all the walls plastered.

Carpentry also accounts for a sizeable portion of your labor costs in home construction. Again, the use of large sheets, such as plywood and hardboard, in certain areas, can greatly reduce labor costs without a sacrifice of building quality. Discuss this phase of economy with the Building Inspector and engineers, and the carpenters whom you hire to do the work.

Painting consumes an estimated 4 per cent of the building fund, but the labor in applying paint accounts for 80 to 85 per cent of the total money spent on this phase. The price difference between the best paints and cheap material is small in comparison to a total application cost. It costs as much to apply cheap paint as it does good paint. Don't be pennywise and pound foolish. Quality paint will last many years longer than will inferior brands. The few extra dollars spent for good material will be well invested, since you won't have the high labor costs of repainting nearly as soon as you would by using cheaper materials.

LAWNS: Immediate consideration must be given to setting in a good lawn. This is more than a beauty factor, because the grass will prevent rain from washing away soil, which might expose plumbing to the weather, and from washing away soil that protects the foundation. This is particularly imperative in a case where land has been filled in at various spots to bring it level, but it also applies to all building spots, since soil has been disturbed when foundation and pipes were installed. This is something you can do yourself, after the hustle and bustle of building has been completed and when the construction crews are no longer using the ground as a traffic area. However, even doing it yourself, figure approximately $200 for seed to plant a 50 x 100 foot lot and adding a few pieces of shrubbery.

PROTECT MATERIAL: It is possible you will suffer as much as 10 to 15 per cent loss of materials cost through pilferage and vandalism, if you are not careful. Both youngsters and teen-agers seem to have a peculiar fascination for buildings under construction. Windows are often broken, plumbing and wiring pulled out, expensive wood, fixtures, and plaster destroyed — all as a result of mischief. Two children, both under 10, recently caused almost $2,000 damage to a house near completion in Michigan — in less than one hour!

Lumber, cement, fixtures, and other supplies that might be stored outside, or in an accessible place, are all game for petty thieves and mischievous children. Frequently, there will be some larceny-minded person who notices the unguarded building, and who immediately plans for the sale of materials he will pick up later that night. Arrange to have your garage or basement fixed, as soon as possible, so that it can be locked — then store your materials under lock and key.

Sand and gravel, left outdoors, causes a different kind of loss. Rains will wash a lot of your materials away. Small children find fun in jumping and kicking around in large piles of sand and gravel—and mixing them up. Such sand and gravel as isn't lost, strayed or stolen, must then be sifted before using, and this requires costly man hours. This material should be stored indoors, under lock and key; or if outdoor storage is the only choice, arrange to have only small quantities delivered, with the balance of the material on a standby basis, available when you need it.

Consult your attorney and insurance agent about obtaining insurance coverage against vandalism and pilferage. Such policies are available, and the premium will be a good investment. Also, consult the local police and request that they give special attention to your building site. They are as anxious to prevent such nefarious and costly activities as you are, and they will cooperate. If you can arrange to run several electric lights onto the building

Tricks in Saving Money When Building

site, and leave them burning all night, this will provide protection against pilferage.

By following the procedures outlined in this chapter, you can build your dream home at a saving of at least 25 per cent. Where off-season buying has been utilized, and a little shopping around done for materials and craftsmen, it is entirely possible to save up to 35 per cent of the total value of the home.

The few months of coordination and buying will amount to cash savings of from $6,000 to $8,000 on a $25,000 home. This shows in a greatly reduced mortgage, since you don't receive cash for your efforts—you merely save it. This money is not considered income, even though it results from your efforts, and it is therefore not taxable.

Perhaps the most rewarding factor in building a home in this way, does not lie in the money saved. It is more that, having figuratively built the home yourself, you will enjoy it far more because of your personal efforts.

BUILDING COST BREAKDOWN CHART

Total value of home	$25,000.00
Architect fee at 5%	1,250.00
Cost of ground	3,750.00
TOTAL TO BE SPENT BUILDING HOME	$20,000.00

Building Phase	Per Cent	Cost
1. Excavation and ground clearance	1%	$ 200.00
2. Concrete and other masonry	8%	1,600.00
3. Lumber	8%	1,600.00
4. Rough carpentry	3%	600.00
5. Insulation	2%	400.00
6. Plumbing	10%	2,000.00
7. Electrical fixtures & labor	6%	1,200.00
8. Heating and air conditioning	8%	1,600.00
9. Sashes, doors, etc.	3%	600.00
10. Roofing	3%	600.00
11. Lathwork and plastering	10%	2,000.00
12. Painting	4%	800.00
13. Tile and hardware	3%	600.00
14. Hardwood floors, other covering	5%	1,000.00
15. Finish carpentry	3%	600.00
16. Kitchen built-ins & cabinets	4%	800.00
17. Miscellaneous (metal work, decorations, lawn, etc.)	4%	800.00
	85%	$17,000.00
18. General contractor, overhead	5%	1,000.00
19. General contractor, profit	10%	2,000.00
	100%	$20,000.00

Style and type construction will cause some of the above figures to vary, however, this percentage breakdown is a typical basic plan.

FREE SERVICES AVAILABLE TO HOME BUILDERS FROM ELECTRIC POWER COMPANIES

State	City	Company	Heat Planning	Inspection of Wiring	Light Planning	Kitchen planning	General Remarks
Ala.	Birmingham	Ala. Power Co.	yes	yes	yes	yes	Pays up to $80 on new electric service entrances. Laundry planning and layout.
Ariz.	Phoenix	Arizona Public Service Co.	yes	yes	yes	yes	Have financing plan.
Calif.	Los Angeles	So. Cal. Edison Co.	yes	—	yes	yes	Home Economists and Lighting consultants.
Colo.	Pueblo	So. Colorado Power Co.	yes	yes	yes	yes	Lighting and Electric consultations.
Colo.	Denver	Public Service Co. of Colo.	re-marks	no	yes	yes	Specialize in gas heat. Lighting specialists.

State	City	Company	Heat Planning	Inspection of Wiring	Light Planning	Kitchen Planning	General Remarks
Conn.	New Haven	United Illuminating Co.	no	yes	yes	yes	Have elaborate home service department.
Del.	Wilmington	Delaware Power & Light Co.	yes	yes	yes	yes	Heating, lighting specialists available.
D.C.	Washington	Potomac Electric Power Co.	no	yes	yes	yes	Survey & estimate elec. heat. Trial lighting.
Fla.	Miami	Florida Power & Light Co.	remarks	remarks	yes	yes	Fla. Home Heating Inst. gives heating advice. City does wiring inspection.
	Pensacola	Gulf Power Co.	no	yes	yes	yes	Garden & patio lighting; laundry lay-out.
	St. Petersburg	Fla. Power Corp.	yes	yes	yes	yes	Numerous professional advisors without charge.

State	City	Company	Heat Planning	Inspection of Wiring	Light Planning	Kitchen Planning	General Remarks
Fla. (cont.)	Tampa	Tampa Electric Co.	yes	yes	yes	yes	Complete free service available.
Ga.	Columbus	Ga. Power Co.	yes	yes	yes	yes	Inspect wiring for adequacy, heat, for capacity
Hawaii	Honolulu	Hawaiian Electric Co.	no	no	yes	yes	Assistance on wiring and outdoor lighting.
Ill.	Chicago	Commonwealth Edison Co.	yes	yes	yes	—	Inspect electric system in homes under construction.
	Decatur	Illinois Power Co.	yes	yes	yes	—	Elec. heating estimates and adequate wiring.
	Peoria	Central Illinois Light Co.	yes	yes	yes	—	Wiring, lighting and elec. heating advisory service.

State	City	Company	Heat Planning	Inspection of Wiring	Light Planning	Kitchen Planning	General Remarks
Ind.	Fort Wayne	Ind. & Mich. Electric Co.	yes	yes	yes	yes	Wiring, lighting and laundry planning services.
Iowa	Davenport	Iowa-Illinois Gas & Electric Co.	yes	yes	–	–	Wiring service, special interest in gas heat.
Kansas	Topeka	Kansas Power & Light Co.	yes	yes	yes	yes	Electric heating, cooking lighting consultants
Kansas	Wichita	Kansas Gas & Electric Co.	yes	yes	yes	yes	Elec. heat and wiring in new homes. Low s
Ky.	Covington	Union Light, Heat & Power Co.	yes	yes	yes	yes	Finances new home wiring. Indoor & outdoor lighting.
Ky.	Lexington	Kentucky Utilities Company	yes	yes	yes	yes	Heat planning and wiring specialists available.

State	City	Company	Heat Planning	Inspection of Wiring	Light Planning	Kitchen Planning	
Maine	Augusta	Central Maine Power Co.	yes	yes	yes	–	Home service. Home heating specialists available.
Md.	Baltimore	Baltimore Gas & Electric Co.	yes	yes	yes	yes	Have elaborate staff of advisors and specialists.
Mass.	Boston	New England Electric System	yes	yes	yes	–	Heat loss survey; have large service staff.
Mich.	Detroit	Detroit Edison Co.	yes	yes	yes	yes	Most elaborate service program in the country.
	Battle Creek Grand Rapids Flint Jackson Kalamazoo	Consumers Power Company	yes	yes	yes	yes	Have complete services available.

State	City	Company	Heat Planning	Inspection of Wiring	Light Planning	Kitchen Planning	General Remarks
Minn.	Minneapolis St. Paul	Northern States Power Co.	yes	yes	yes	yes	Specialists available for heating and lighting.
Miss.	Jackson	Mississippi Power & Light Co.	yes	yes	yes	–	Home lighting and engineering services.
Nebr.	Omaha	Omaha Public Power Dist.	–	re- marks	yes	–	Inspect wiring outside city limits.
N. J.	Camden Jersey City Newark Paterson Trenton	Public Service Electric & Gas Co.	yes	yes	yes	yes	New home wiring inspected free, also need city inspection. Other advisory services available.
N. Y.	New York	Con. Edison Co. of N.Y., Inc.	yes	yes	yes	yes	Advise on wiring, have staff of specialists.

State	City	Company	Heat Planning	Inspection of Wiring	Light Planning	Kitchen Planning	General Remarks
N. C.	Charlotte	Duke Power Co.	yes	yes	yes	yes	Lighting engineers and home economists services.
N. D.	Fargo	Northern States Power Co.	yes	yes	yes	yes	Have many services available, including laundry.
Ohio	Cleveland	Cleveland Illuminating Electric Co.	yes	yes	yes	yes	Electric heating and wiring advice free.
	Columbus	Columbus & So. Ohio Electric Co.	yes	yes	yes	yes	Wiring, lighting, heating, air conditioning service.
	Dayton	Dayton Power & Light Co.	yes	yes	yes	yes	Many specialist services available.

State	City	Company	Heat Planning	Inspection of Wiring	Light Planning	Kitchen Planning	General Remarks
Pa.	Pittsburgh	Duquesne Light Co.	yes	yes	yes	yes	Heating, insulation, wiring and general services.
R. I.	Newport	Newport Electric Corp.	–	yes	yes	yes	Have various specialists available.
	Providence	Narragansett Electric Co.	yes	yes	–	–	Specialize in electric heated homes.
S. D.	Rapid City	Black Hills Power & Light Co.	yes	yes	yes	yes	Counselors and specialists on electrical problems.
	Sioux Falls	Northern States Power Co.	yes	yes	yes	yes	General advisory staff, plan home laundries.
Tenn.	Chattanooga	Electric Power Board of Chattanooga	yes	yes	yes	yes	Finance new home wiring, have general advisory services.

State	City	Company	Heat Planning	Inspection of Wiring	Light Planning	Kitchen Planning	General Remarks
Tenn. (cont.)	Knoxville	Knoxville Utilities Board	yes	yes	yes	yes	Free heating and wiring advice and assistance.
	Nashville	Nashville Electric Service	yes	yes	yes	yes	Free advice on light and heating.
Texas	Beaumont	Gulf States Utilities Co.	yes	yes	yes	yes	Have large staff of advisors. Finance wiring.
	Corpus Christi	Central Power & Light Co.	yes	yes	yes	yes	General electrical advice. Air conditioning planning.
	El Paso	El Paso Electric Co.	yes	yes	yes	yes	Many services available.

State	City	Company	Heat Planning	Inspection of Wiring	Light Planning	Kitchen Planning	General Remarks
Texas (cont.)	Forth Worth	Texas Electric Service Co.	yes	yes	yes	yes	General electrical service including outdoor.
	Lubbock	Lubbock Municipal Power & Light Co.	yes	yes	yes	yes	Specialists in almost all electrical uses.
	San Antonio	City Public Service Board	yes	yes	yes	yes	General electrical advice. Outdoor light planning.
Vermont	Burlington	Burlington Electric Light Dept.	yes	–	–	–	Inspect electrically heated homes.
Wash.	Spokane	The Washington Water Power Co.	yes	yes	yes	yes	Specialize in building, remodeling services.

State	City	Company	Heat Planning	Inspection of Wiring	Light Planning	Kitchen Planning	General Remarks
Wash. (cont.)	Tacoma	Dept. of Public Welfare	yes	yes	yes	yes	Have large staff of specialists and counselors.
Wisc.	LaCrosse	Northern States Power Co.	yes	yes	yes	yes	Full consulting service, including laundry planning.

Chapter 9

WHAT TO DO BEFORE - DURING - AND AFTER MOVING

Probably, one of the biggest problems you will encounter in taking possession of your new home is the actual process of moving. Although an estimated 35 million Americans move each year, many of them still run into problems, including unnecessary losses, expenses and physical injury, simply because they aren't prepared for the task.

The problemof moving is just as great for a two-block haul as for several hundred miles. If you do your own packing, or do the entire moving job yourself, there are many pitfalls and precautions that must be considered. Even when a complete professional moving service is employed, and you simply walk out of the old house, letting the movers pack the dishes and all the rest, there are still many things that must be attended to.

Unless considerable caution is used in making arrangements with the moving company, closely balanced budgets can be destroyed. Definite figures should be obtained on the total cost before the agreement is signed; then, insist that the company sign the final agreement showing total costs. In some instances it will not be possible to fix an exact cost prior to moving, but in such cases you should insist that the estimate be submitted <u>in writing.</u>

Because so many complaints were received, the Michigan State Public Service Commission recently found it necessary to conduct a full scale investigation into the business practices of moving companies. One witness testified that he received four different estimates, from as many companies, for a local move. The estimated prices ranged from $72 to $144 on the job, and he selected a well-known and established company offering an estimate of $85. When the move was completed, he received a bill for $314, at which time he discovered that he had neglected to secure anything in writing as to the original estimate, so he had to pay the exorbitant bill.

What to do Before - During - and After Moving

This is such a general practice that one of the leading national moving firms advertises: "Regardless of any prior estimate received for the carriage of your shipment, you will be required to pay transportation charges and other charges computed in accordance with tariffs filed by the carrier with the Interstate Commerce Commission, plus transportation tax. The total charges which you will be required to pay may be more, or less, than the estimate received from the carrier."

To further compound the situation of the Michigan man, several losses were incurred during the moving, for which the company was not liable, even though they advertise they are "fully insured." A little advance thought and sound business dealing, resulting in fully estimated costs in writing, would prevent such situations.

Remember that moving is a cash proposition. Before the men start unloading at your new address, the driver will insist on payment in cash or certified check, unless other arrangements have been definitely made with the company. Make sure you have the cash ready, because if you don't, they can put the furniture into transit storage with a minimum 30 day charge, plus the added cost of moving it from the warehouse back to your home after payment is made. If they are made to wait while you secure the money, you will be charged the full hourly rate for all the men assigned to that van, during the time they have been made to wait for payment.

The chart below will provide an approximate idea of average costs on a weight-mileage basis. Short, local moves are generally computed on an hourly rate, with prices varying according to the number of men assigned to the van, so they do not apply. An additional 50 cents per 100 dollars of value should be added to these figures for additional insurance, and $1.50 per 100 pounds for packing service, if such a service is to be used.

MOVING INSURANCE: Compare insurance coverage and rates carefully. For moves involving less than 700 miles, a cargo—or transit—insurance policy, available through local brokers and agents, is probably your best bet, since it gives comparable coverage, and costs less than the usual insurance supplied by moving companies. For longer moves, one of the

Miles	2 Rooms	3 Rooms	4 Rooms	5 Rooms	6 Rooms
50	$ 65	$ 95	$110	$140	$160
100	75	110	125	160	190
200	100	150	165	200	240
300	120	180	195	240	290
500	160	240	260	320	385
1000	235	255	400	500	590
1500	300	450	525	660	790
2000	350	530	660	820	985

"protection plans" offered by most large companies will probably be the best buy.

Under most conditions, the moving company is legally liable for only 30 to 50 cents per pound on every article being moved, with the limit of liability varying in different areas. This actually isn't an insurance rule—it is merely the carrier's stipulation that he doesn't assume responsibility for more than this specified amount. When you accept this base rate, and sign the bill of lading, you go on record as agreeing to these conditions. Many companies advertise that they are "fully insured" but this really doesn't mean a thing—so don't be misled by such exaggerated claims. Most reputable moving companies, however, will provide full protection for a flat rate, regardless of the distance involved. The usual fee is 50 cents for each $100 of declared value. Check the moving companies' rates for full coverage, then compare the rates and protection with your individual insurance broker, to determine which provides best protection, and which proves best from the dollar standpoint.

No matter what form of insurance you finally select, <u>read the small print carefully</u>! Most contracts have some restrictions. Practically all contracts <u>exclude</u> damage to fragile goods, such as china, glassware, mirrors, etc., <u>if you packed them yourself</u>! Almost all contracts deny responsibility for loss of jewelry, money, securities and other valuables lost through "mysterious disappearance." Another point for close attention is that movers seldom accept responsibility for the malfunctioning of appliances that require special servicing, such as stoves, refrigerators, TV sets, etc., <u>unless</u> you have had them serviced by a qualified serviceman before the mover arrives.

Whether you carry special insurance or not, there are some points for which the mover automatically must assume full responsibility. He is, for instance, fully responsible for damage to property caused by the negligence or carelessness of his employees. Should the van run over a hedge while backing into the driveway, an employee walk through a flower bed, or plaster be chipped from a wall, or a glass broken, while furniture is being moved, such acts—and others of this nature—are the full responsibility of the movers. They will settle such claims without argument, provided they are notified at the time of occurrence, or immediately thereafter.

<u>BEFORE YOU MOVE</u>: Make arrangements with the moving company at least 10 days in advance; then, avoid confusion by calling the day before the move, to confirm the exact time the van will arrive. Have all laundry clean so as to avoid this chore while getting established in your new home. Send out such clothing as needs cleaning, and have it delivered to your new address if you are moving within the same city. Prepare meals a few days in advance and put them in the freezer; and have a shopping list ready for the few little necessary things you'll need at your new location to get the kitchen in efficient operation.

Moving, when there are children in the family, can either be a smooth operation with a promise of new adventure for youngsters, or a nightmare of confusion, uncertainty and resentment. Where parents are tense, confused and worried, the children will immediately sense this state—which can cause unhappiness and a feeling of insecurity for them. Moving plans should be discussed with children well in advance of the big day. Give them the reason for the move, and encourage them to talk about it, so that they won't feel left out. Assigning a few small tasks to them will create the feeling of being part of the family move—and, of course, whenever possible, plans should be made to avoid changing schools during terms, so that, by the time they do start at the new school, they will have had time to meet some of the other children.

Where children are old enough, allow them to inspect the new home, and show them where their new room will be situated. Also, allowing them to plan the color scheme and furniture arrangement of their room will add much to the adventure of the move.

Before moving is the ideal time to conduct a mass house cleaning and throwing-away campaign. Even in apartments, the average family collects many items, over the years, for which there will never again be a need—and the time to weed out such unnecessary things is before moving. Why clutter up the new home with needless objects, and why pay to have such items packed and shipped? For instance, an old piano might cost much more to crate and move than it is actually worth. Return items borrowed from neighbors, and collect things they might have that belong to you. If you are taking rugs, drapes, etc., with you, this is the perfect time to send them to the cleaners, having them delivered to the new address just before the moving van arrives. Arrange for pets to be boarded out for a few days, to allow time for settling.

Make a diagram of the floor plan in the new home, mark it to show where each piece of furniture should be placed, and give this to the moving men. Mark each carton you pack to show where it should go in the new home, and put up signs in each room of the new place, designating the place where you want each piece of furniture. This will not only save the time (which means money in hourly rates) of the moving men, but will eliminate the necessity of having to move heavy furniture around after the van has left. When moves are made in winter, make sure all sidewalks are cleared of snow—a practice which, again, makes moving faster and saves you money in hourly rates.

Furthermore, prepare your washer, dryer, freezer, refrigerator, and other appliances by bracing the motors as recommended in the service manual. Unless you are sure about how it should be done, it will pay to have a serviceman do the job. This is also a good time to have faulty appliances sent out and repaired, with delivery made to the new home. Defrost the refrigerator before

What to do Before - During - and After Moving

starting a move which involves a long haul. Pack books in small, strong boxes back to back; limit cartons to not more than 50 pounds, and make sure they are securely tied. Group articles that will be used in one room, so that unpacking and settling will be that much easier.

Carefully check the list below to insure that none of the little —but still important—necessary prerequisites to moving have not been overlooked. Forgetting even the smallest steps at this point can cause great inconvenience, be costly in time and money, and disrupt your family life.

UTILITIES

Gas and Electric — Arrange to have services disconnected at a time immediately <u>after</u> you move, since electricity will be needed during course of moving. Also arrange for service to begin at your new home just <u>before</u> the van arrives, since you also need electricity at the new home <u>during</u> moving.

Water — Make similar arrangements with water for both old and new houses. Make sure water is turned off at old house if move is made during freezing weather.

Telephone — Leave phone service on until after entire move is completed, then call company for a disconnect. Have new service started an hour <u>before</u> the move begins, as you might want to communicate with other family members from the new location, during moving.

Fuel Oil — Notify company servicing your fuel, of the moving date, so they can check both the new and old addresses. If the same company is going to service your new home, an allowance can probably be effected for the fuel supply left at old address.

Water Softener	Where conditioning units are leased, the company must be notified, as you are responsible. Credit for old unit will be given on one installed at your new home.
Garbage Service	Where contractual garbage service is used, they must be notified to discontinue at old address and start at new one.

FINANCIAL RESPONSIBILITIES

Charge Accounts	Notify all places where you have charge accounts or credit cards of change of address. This should be done about five days in advance of your move.
Bank Accounts	Notify bank of move and have them transfer your accounts to a more convenient branch. They can also arrange for a bonded messenger to deliver contents of safe deposit boxes to the new bank. Make sure you have sufficient cash, travelers checks, or a certified check to cover moving costs, as personal checks are not acceptable. Get a credit reference from your bank if moving to another city.
Insurance	Notify all insurance companies at least five days in advance of address change. Be particularly alert to the fire, theft and burglary policies, so that they go into effect at new address on the moving day. Include Social Security and Veterans Administration in your notifications, as required.

HOUSEHOLD DUTIES

Milk Service	Notify the milkman; his company probably services your new location, and the account can be transferred.

What to Do Before - During - and After Moving

Newspapers	If your move is within the same city, your present service can be transferred to coincide with the move.
Magazines	Notify all publishing houses with whom you have subscriptions six weeks in advance of move, if possible.
Laundry	Laundry, dry cleaning, and diaper services should be notified several days in advance, so they can pick up at new home without delay.

FAMILY OBLIGATIONS

Post Office	Send in change-of-address cards at least five days in advance of move. It takes a few days for the change to become effective, so don't wait until the last minute.
Medical	Have your family doctor recommend a physician in the new neighborhood, if your doctor doesn't service that same area.
Church	If moving away from present parish, have church suggest one in new neighborhood, and request that the new priest or person be contacted.
School	Obtain a transcript of your children's school records from present school, to avoid delay and confusion in new enrollment.
Friends	Notify all friends of new address and telephone number. <u>Your last years' Christmas card list is a good guide for this job</u>, along with your address book.

<u>DURING THE MOVE</u>: Carry jewelry, cash, securities and other valuables with you, or send some ahead by registered mail. Although moving companies might advertise that they are fully insured, there is a small clause in their contracts which

definitely relieves them of responsibility from "mysterious disappearances." Special handling should also be given to antiques and other exceptionally valuable items, since many companies pay damages only on a poundage basis, regardless of actual value. Under such conditions, without specific personal insurance, if a valuable lamp or vase were broken, you might be allowed only a few dollars on the weight of the object, rather than on its true value.

Whenever possible, it is advisable to leave children with relatives or close friends during the actual moving process. When this is not practical, keep them close to you, and out of the way. Prepare a separate bag of formula, diapers, etc. for baby, and carry this with you. Keep a few favorite toys or games to amuse the very young, since the increased activity might frighten them. Pack another basket with toilet articles that you will require immediately upon arrival at the new home, plus sandwiches and a Thermos of coffee or other beverage, which can be put into instant use once you arrive at the new address. Have the moving men dismantle furniture from the children's room last, so that it can be reassembled in the new home first. Seeing their own furniture slip into place so quickly will give children reassurance that the move is not going to be harmful to them.

Check furniture, appliances, and household items as they are brought into the new home, and be sure to note any damage or loss on the bill of lading before you sign the form. When loss or damage is discovered, give personal notice to the company at once, in addition to noting it on the shipping form. Request an inspection of the damage, or an investigation of the loss, <u>immediately</u>. If these things are allowed to go without a strong push, they frequently become lost in the shuffle. Sign the shipping form only after you are satisfied with the move, or have adequately noted discrepancies.

<u>AFTER THE MOVE:</u> If you paid for packing services, the same price includes unpacking, so take the family out to eat, while the men perform their jobs. If not, don't try to do everything at once. Get rooms ready for the children, and the kitchen in working order, as soon as possible without causing confusion. Sit down for a few minutes with the children and let them talk

about the big day, allowing them to make suggestions about what's to be done next. Encourage children to play outdoors, and to bring new-found friends home, even though the house may be in a state of disorder. The sooner they become acquainted with other children, the quicker they will overcome whatever trauma they may have experienced through being uprooted at the old home. With teen-age children, insist that they invite some friends from the old neighborhood over as soon as the house is in order, for adolescent children need as much reassurance and acceptance as younger ones during the period of such a drastic change in their way of life.

Check the fuse box to determine that previous owners haven't installed fuses that are too heavy, or have put pennies behind fuses. Such things can cause fires; so, make sure *proper* fuses are installed in all circuits. Check all appliances; and have the serviceman come in, if necessary, to guarantee that everything is working perfectly. Call utility companies, household services, and close friends to let them know you are finally settled. Check with the postal carrier, to see if there is any mail being held for you.

IF YOU DO YOUR OWN PACKING: The easiest way to move, of course, is simply to turn over the keys to the new and old houses, along with floor plans and directions, to professional movers—then take a week's vacation. Unfortunately, such a luxury is expensive, and most families prefer doing at least part of the job to cut down cost. One of the biggest mistakes made by budget-conscious families is to pack linens, bedding, clothing, etc., into bureau drawers instead of into cartons. By overloading expensive furniture in this manner, more weight is added than the drawers and frames are designed to hold. Bottoms, backs, or fronts of drawers may be forced out of position, often necessitating expensive repairs. Lightweight pillows and hats may be packed into bureau drawers, but other, heavier items should be strictly confined to cartons. Also, remove casters from furniture, place them in bags, and put bags inside drawers so that they may be quickly assembled at the new location.

Line sturdy paperboard cartons with clean, white paper. The use of newspaper is not recommended, since the ink print will rub off, sometimes causing permanent stains. Pack items in layers, not to exceed 50 pounds per carton; seal cartons with gummed tape, and paste an identification sticker on the outside so that you instantly locate the enclosed items when unpacking. Use either shredded paper or excelsior when packing china and dishes. It is best to slightly dampen shredded paper first, so that it conforms to the shape of each item, giving maximum protection. Pack dishes standing on edge—never flat—in the boxes. Always keep contents of boxes below the inside edge, allowing the cartons to be stacked onto each other to facilitate loading. Place the heaviest items at the bottoms of boxes and do not mix breakables with nonbreakable materials in the same container. Label all boxes that contain glass or other fragile material. Suitcases and satchels take up as much room empty as they do full, so use them for packing purposes. Kit bags, hunting knapsacks, etc., may also be utilized for packing odds and ends, and unbreakable objects.

Drain any equipment that might leak during transit, ruining expensive furniture or clothing. Never pack an engine or power tools in shredded paper, as the paper might foul the motor. Remove batteries from any battery-powered tools, toys or other equipment. Leave tubes in radios and TV sets, and do not attempt packing cushioning material around them. Tape down arms of record players, and remove all records from spindle. Pack records separately, standing on edges, with padding between each one.

Moves made within the same city are usually billed on the number of man hours required to complete the job—not on the distance. In the interest of economy, pack as many cartons as possible on the ground floor of your house, enabling the moving men to make quick trips to the van, thus saving costly man-hours. But be sure to leave sufficient space to allow the men to maneuver larger objects, which might best be loaded onto the van first.

Another very common, and quite expensive, mistake made by those packing or moving by themselves, is to roll mattresses. A sheet or mattress cover should be left on, and the mattress packed in a large carton especially designed by moving companies for this purpose. Rolling mattresses often results in springs pulling loose, the outer fabric being torn, and the general usefulness of the expensive mattress is being destroyed.

Packing flammables and partially filled containers of liquids is another, costly mistake. It is far better to waste small quantities of flammables, acids or other liquids, than to take a chance of their spilling, causing damage to expensive furniture, furnishings or clothing—or possibly burning up the entire van. Also, be especially cautious in packing matches or lighter fluids which can cause fires. Both are easy to throw away and later replace. Large framed pictures, mirrors, and marble or glass table tops should be individually crated and carefully padded with excelsior, blankets, or regular shipping mats.

DOING YOUR OWN MOVING: If you plan on doing the actual moving yourself, bear in mind that this is a time consuming, tiresome job, so allow yourself sufficient time for a series of small moves, rather than trying it all in a few hours—or even in one day. The family car may be used to transport breakable items and small pieces of furniture and cartons. Several trips, each evening before the big moving day, will take a great strain out of the actual move. Trailers may be rented for medium-sized goods that can withstand fairly rough treatment, since these trailers are not designed for smooth riding and do sometimes cause damage to fine furniture. On the day of moving, rent a small van or truck, some furniture padding, a loading ramp, and a dolly for heavy furniture and appliances. Then, gather your friends and distribute object weight so that no one person handles the equivalent of more than 75 pounds at a time. In other words, if the object weighs 225 pounds, make sure there are at least three people sharing the load weight.

Moving objects to your new home piecemeal will require someone's staying at the new address to protect such furnishings, so take a bed along with you on the first load. Also, consult your insurance broker about the possibility of securing some insurance, both from theft and damage standpoints.

Chapter 10

LEARNING TO LIVE WITH YOUR NEW HOME

New homes, like new cars, must go through a "breaking in" period when special attention and some care are required.

Many people have the impression that just because a house is newly constructed, no work will be needed; this is nonsense. Every house needs some care and work. Older buildings may require major surgery, while new ones can be competently handled with a little preventive medicine, but they all require some treatment. Since 3,000 component parts, plus about 650 pounds of nails, plus other fixtures and hardware, go into the making of a 1,200-square-foot house, it is certainly possible that some materials may have been slightly below par, and that installation may have been a trifle irregular. A slight margin of error or defect in any phase of construction will require some adjustment or maintenance to bring about the desired good building.

Even if every component part had been expertly installed, perfect in condition and cut, you would still have the "terrible trio" with which to contend: shrinkage, settling and swelling. The builder or parts manufacturer has absolutely no control over these three conditions, which are to be found in every house. They are situations the homeowner must learn to recognize, accept and control.

Unless you are prepared to accept such conditions, the first year in your new home may become a complete nightmare. Once you recognize the inevitable, know the reason for these conditions, and learn how to correct them, there is no real problem. Getting through the first year may be a little troublesome at times, but, with a cool head and common sense, you'll emerge with flying colors, able to enjoy the home far more, during years to come, for having had such experiences during the first year's "breaking in" period.

It is your right to expect the builder to take care of large or serious troubles during that first year, and honest, competent builders allow for such maintenance in the over-all cost. However, they are not legally responsible for many of the little irregularities with which you'll be confronted. A friendly relationship with the builder can be completely destroyed by your running to him with every minor complaint. He builds many houses, and your small complaints (most of which are not his responsibility), multiplied, can run into enormous costs for him. In a case where the homeowner doesn't make his own minor repairs, the easiest way of handling them is to keep a running list, wait until there's enough work to keep a craftsman busy for at least a couple of hours, then, submit the entire list to the builder. If there is at least one major complaint, builders will usually honor such lists, and take care of minor problems, even though the homeowner is responsible for "normal maintenance." In other cases, builders will send in an experienced man to handle minor defects, making charges only for the hourly wage and the parts used. Look over your Builder's Construction Guarantee—which in most cases clearly outlines the responsibility of the builder—and try to hold your first year's complaints within reasonable limits.

BUILDER'S RESPONSIBILITY

At the time of settlement, insist that the builder give you a guarantee on all construction, including plumbing, heating, the electrical system, and the foundation construction—for at least one year. If a home has been purchased under a FHA mortgage, the builder is compelled to provide a warranty that all materials and workmanship conform to the approved specifications. If nationally known products have been used in construction, the manufacturer usually supplies a guarantee with mechanical equipment such as the furnace, water heater, dishwasher, garbage disposal, etc. National brand-names on floors, doors, tiles and similar items also usually provide a guarantee, both on the product and the work. You should receive such warranties and guarantees at the time of settlement. If you don't, ask for them before the final payment is made.

ing and "giving," but this is another natural phase in a new home.

You should be entirely familiar with all the clauses in your building contract. Generally the builder guarantees that all work will be done in a "good and workmanlike manner"—an ambiguous sounding phrase, but one which does protect you against an out-and-out shoddy or inefficient job. So, insist that such a phrase appear in your contract.

THE TERRIBLE TRIO

<u>SETTLING</u> You must remember that even small houses weigh 2 tons or more, concentrated on a small piece of ground, so it is inevitable that the soil below must give, to some degree—and when the soil gives, the house settles. In rare cases, when everything settles evenly, no one notices the process, but since the soil is bound to be softer in certain spots, and the load heavier in other places, some foundation sections sink more rapidly than others, causing uneven settling, and structural cracks then appear. Don't be alarmed when this occurs; it happens to all new houses, and minor cracks around windows and at corners do not affect the strength of the walls. Such cracks are unpleasant to see, but they are very easy to fix.

Another factor that must be considered about your home, before you start blaming the builder or materials, is a wide variation in temperatures. Since the building's foundation <u>base</u> is below frost line, it generally maintains an even temperature of about 56 degrees, while the foundation's exposed parts are subjected to temperatures varying between zero in winter and 100 degrees or more in summer. Therefore, such a drastic difference, the expansion and contraction is sometimes quite radical, and structural cracks are bound to appear. So, accept the fact that cracks will start appearing during the first year, and take them in stride.

You will also probably notice cracks appearing where the bathtub and wall join, but this is a normal settling condition that you can correct by scraping out the old calk and applying a new bead with calking tubes—obtainable in all hardware stores, complete with grouting tip, for less than a cent a foot of calk.

Learning to Live with your New Home

SHRINKAGE Even in the most expensive houses, rough framing lumber is usually not completely dry, since fully cured materials for this stage of construction would add considerably to the total building cost. When rough framing begins to dry out because of the heat within the house, uneven shrinkage occurs, and you may end up with cracks in your plastered walls and ceilings. This process usually takes about two years, so immediate repairs are not recommended, as the cracks will probably widen before the two-year period is up. After that period, cracks may be effectively repaired with spackling or patching plaster.

You may also find cracks developing at ceiling, window, and door moldings during especially dry weather. Again, don't worry, for this also happens to most new homes. These cracks will probably close themselves in humid weather, but if they don't, fill them with calk or putty after the first year, then patch-paint those particular sections. The calk or putty, retaining some degree of resilience, will flex with the normal expansion and contraction caused by humidity. Excessive shrinkage can be best controlled by keeping the indoor temperature around 70 degrees during the first year. Higher temperatures will cause the house to dry out too fast.

When you start using your fireplace, the extreme heat will probably cause brick mortar to dry out rapidly, which will result in cracks appearing where the fireplace joins the wall, or perhaps even between bricks. Wait until the heating season is over; then scrape and tuck point all cracks.

SWELLING In your new home, you can expect some doors and windows to stick. It's a rare house, indeed, that goes through the first year without this particular malady. Even thoroughly conditioned doors, competently fitted before hanging, have a tendency to swell during damp weather, and if this situation reaches a stage that causes inconvenience, lightly sand the high spots. The use of a plane is not recommended since doors will probably shrink back to normal size during dry weather; and, if they have been heavily planed to smooth out the swell spots, they will develop a loose fit once the damp weather has passed.

Wood flooring automatically goes through a period of squeak-

It is impossible to have a perfectly tight floor, all year round, in a new house. Without the hairline cracks in the flooring during the winter months, floors would buckle during the humid summer months. As the house settles, and the expansion and contraction reduces to a minimum, this condition generally corrects itself. However, if you notice the floor sagging in the middle, check the bracing on the underside, and, if braces have pulled loose, nail them securely back into position.

Uneven settling of soil around the foundation often causes moisture conditions in basements. This can be one of the most discouraging first-year complaints, but it is not necessarily a serious matter. Often, the soil, sinking around the foundation, pitches water toward the foundation instead of away from it; then the misdirected water pockets, and eventually seeps through the basement walls. As long as there are no cracks in the basement walls, be patient with this new home malady, and allow the soil to settle completely.

After several good rains, walk around the house, examining the juncture where the ground joints the wall. There should be at least a 10 degree pitch of the soil to throw water _away_ from the building. If depressions are noticed, a few loads of dirt will usually correct this seemingly impossible situation, and you can enjoy a dry basement.

Cracks in basement walls should receive close observation. If they seem to become larger, they should be called to the builder's attention at once. Because basement walls are colder than the warm interior air, they are quick to show condensation beads, so don't mistake this for a leaking problem. Opening a basement window during dry days, closing it during humid days, will usually correct this condition. Provide ample ventilation when the laundry is being done, or when clothes are hung in the basement, since this adds an enormous amount of moisture to interior air—and make sure the automatic dryer is properly vented. Sweating pipes can be kept under control by a wrapping of insulation material.

GENERAL BUILDER LIABILITY

If you have made proper negotiations and agreements with the builder, you can expect him either to make repairs or to stand

Learning to Live with your New Home

the expense on major building defects which develop within the first year. The list below highlights some major defects which would justifiably be the builder's responsibility.

<u>FOUNDATION CRACKS</u> Small hairline cracks are not unusual, as this can happen to the best of buildings during the settling process. If they are scraped out and pointed up after the first year, they will probably not reappear. However, if cracks continue to widen, and reach a size where you can insert the point of a pencil, they should be brought to the builder's attention. This could indicate that footings have not been properly laid, and the corrective procedure might be costly.

In slab or basementless houses, where footings have not been put in below the frost line, or where other poor work has been done on footing installation, the foundation may twist in the settling process. A good indication of this major defect is the appearance of horizontal cracks in the foundation wall. If these signs are detected, demand corrective procedure from the builder. Horizontal cracks about halfway up the foundation wall may mean that the walls are not of sufficient thickness, or that they were made from poor concrete mix, and both of these problems are the builder's responsibility.

<u>CEILINGS AND WALLS</u> You may expect small cracks in plaster ceilings and walls, which can be satisfactorily filled after the first year. Cracks that continue to widen, or become big enough to accept a pencil point, should be shown to the builder. These might result from excessive settling, the use of too-green construction lumber that is now pulling apart, or the use of insufficient load-bearing studs. Make the builder take care of such repairs, as they can be expensive, and should be made within the first year. Cracks in walls that form "maps" or "crazing" patterns, indicate either that the plaster was poorly bonded, or that the plaster mix was too rich, or that it dried too fast. It will probably have to be replaced, so make this condition known to the builder and have him correct the defect before the one-year warranty period expires.

<u>INTERIOR CONCRETE FLOORS</u> Interior concrete floors should be a minimum of three inches thick. If flooring cracks

appear, it's a good indication that the builder probably skimped, failing to meet the minimum 3-inch thickness requirement. These cracks could also result from pouring the concrete on dirt that later settled and no longer supports it. Such cracks, serious warning flags of more trouble to come, should be brought to the builder's attention, and correction should be made as soon as possible. If floor cracks radiate from middle-of-the-house posts or piers, the supports are probably resting on the floor slab, instead of on a separate sturdy footing, which should be at least 24 inches square and 12 inches deep. When there is doubt as to floor thickness, a hole can be tapped with a star drill, and the thickness measured.

ROOF Ceiling cracks along the bottom of attic knee walls indicate that the roof is not rigid enough. If knee walls help support the roof, the weight of snow and the pressure of winds will bear directly on the joists under the knee walls. If plaster cracks at this point, or joints have a tendency to separate, have the builder correct the condition.

FLOORS Floors sometimes buckle when they have been improperly laid, without allowance for a small amount of expansion and contraction. Wise builders store flooring material indoors for several days at 70 degrees temperature, and at normal humidity, before installing, allowing the moisture content to adjust to indoor conditions. Frequently, when this isn't done, flooring will buckle unless sufficient expansion room has been allowed. This is definitely the builder's responsibility, and he should either correct the condition or pay for your flooring.

A partition placed over one supporting joist, or on a subflooring without joist support, will cause floors to sag and cracks to appear at the joint where the partition wall intersects another wall. Unless diagonal subflooring or plywood has been used on second story flooring, a cracking condition may develop around the baseboard. The builder is responsible for such inferior building, so make him correct the defect.

WALLS Rigid walls should have studs doubled at all openings and tripled at all corners. If wall sheathing is other than plywood or diagonal boards, braces should be cut into the studs

Learning to Live with your New Home

at corners. If this is not done, you can be almost sure of cracking plaster, so, if plaster starts cracking in excessive amounts, check this building factor, and have the builder make indicated repairs and replacements. When cracks appear where walls meet ceilings, it is usually the result of excessive expansion and contraction of the plate on top of the wall studding. Such a condition on the second floor may be caused by a poorly ventilated attic collecting moisture in the winter, drying out in the summer. Excessive drying of rough lumber framing can also cause such cracks, which may be corrected through maintaining proper humidity inside the house.

WARPING DOORS   Exterior doors pose a serious problem since the outside may be facing zero degrees weather in winter, while the inside has a comfortable 70- to 75-degree heat. Such drastic differences often cause improperly seasoned doors to warp. Should you notice that doors have become so warped or buckled that you can see light through the side where the door meets the jamb, then insist that the builder make the replacement at his expense.

WET BASEMENT   All building contracts should contain a specific clause guaranteeing no outside water seeping into the basement. Since this is a frequent new house malady, many builders will try to avoid this clause if they can, but they will include it if the buyer insists. Wherever a condition exists in which water comes through the floor or walls, it is the builder's liability, and correction should be demanded before the condition becomes too serious and causes other damage. Many times it is simply a matter of holes not having been properly sealed in walls that pipe passes through. Or, it could be faulty foundation construction, which will be extremely expensive to repair.

HEATING SYSTEM   Most heating systems come with a six-month or one-year guarantee, such written warranty being given to you at the time of settlement. Since it is difficult for the installation men to adjust the unit exactly to your needs, at least one service call is expected during the first year. Your system should provide sufficient heat to keep any room at a constant 70 degree temperature on the coldest winter day, and if it does not perform this task, have the servicemen look the plant over. Slight adjustment of the convectors, radiators or registers usually gives the desired result, providing a sufficient heating plant has been installed.

APPLIANCES   Refrigerators, stoves, washers, dryers, dishwashers, air conditioners, garbage disposals, etc. are all guaranteed by the manufacturer and you should receive a written warranty on each of these items at the time of settlement. Keep all such warranties in one place, so that they can be easily got hold of, should some appliances begin malfunctioning. Remember, there is a time limit on all guarantees, so do have defects corrected as soon as they are discovered.

Chapter 11

A GUIDE TO DECORATING YOUR NEW HOME

Anyone buying or building a home, or anyone who contemplates remodeling, or even redecorating, is faced with the seeming insurmountable problem of selecting a color scheme compatible with the family and neighborhood. Modern paints are made to last for many years, so your selection of colors must be good, as you'll be living with them a long time. A poor choice of colors may minimize the pleasures of a home, and can cause clashes and disharmony in a family. Planning colors can be fun—even exciting—but like a game, you only derive maximum benefit from such planning when you know all the rules.

There are two important basic rules involved in good color selection. First, the psychological properties of color in relation to your family must be considered; secondly, the fundamental components should be understood.

You are far better qualified to make your color selections than the most eminent interior decorator, since it's your home—and you'll have to live in it. With a proper color selection, through family participation, you can make your house a pleasant, enjoyable place, and because it is your home, you and your family are the only ones who can really decide on the colors you'll find mutually agreeable to have around.

During recent years, psychologists have definitely determined that colors have individual personalities, and when they are used indiscriminately in a house, they often clash with family personalities. A home is a place in which to relax, enjoy life, and maintain emotional stability. Emotions depend on environment, of which color is one of the most important elements, so, incompatible and irritating colors can actually create emotional upsets.

For instance, as an example of the effect color has on humans, it has been proved that rooms painted in certain shades of red or orange cause some people to suffer from persistent thirst. Babies don't nap well in a yellow nursery, because the color creates an alert atmosphere, while blue will relax them—yet their preference in toys is toward bright red. Farmers seldom prefer green, while factory workers often choose it as a favorite color. Deep blue rooms are depressing; vivid yellow rooms cause headaches; bright red rooms are nerve wracking, and leaf-green rooms are boring. Most men prefer blue, while women have a predominant preference for red. Based on such findings, experts strongly advise one's using no color disliked by any family member. To disregard this psychological factor may cause disharmony in the family—and complete dissatisfaction with the home.

Now, however—without becoming involved in technical aspects—let's take a look at color, and decide how its various characteristics can work with you, and for you. Colors, requiring no room, can create the illusion of roominess. Though inanimate they have definite personalities and character, and the correct colors for you, your home, and family are no more expensive than those that will prove upsetting. Furthermore, once you become acquainted with colors, you can use them as friends.

<u>Primary Colors</u>, red, yellow, blue, are so called because all other colors can be made with them. Black and white are also included in this category. In their pure form, the primary colors are usually too strong to use on large areas, and should therefore be employed with secondaries.

<u>Secondaries</u> are green, orange and purple, which are made by mixing two of the primaries.

<u>Intermediate</u> colors, red-orange, yellow-orange, yellow-green, blue-green, blue-purple and red-purple, are next in the color line-up.

<u>Hues</u> are the primary colors and their mixtures.
<u>Tints</u> are hues, with the addition of white.
<u>Shades</u> are hues, with the addition of black.
<u>Tones</u> are hues, plus both black and white.

An unlimited number of hues can be created by varying proportions and combinations of primary colors. The addition of black or white, or both, to any hue, produces an infinite number of shades, tints and tones. This supplies an unbounded selection of color which can be used to meet the personal requirements of you and your family.

Colors are also classified as warm or cool.

<u>Warm colors</u> are red, orange, yellow. They give the impression of advancing toward you, conveying the feeling of warmth and emotional stimulation. Because they do have this quality of seeming to come toward you, they are ideal for use in large rooms where a feeling of intimacy is desired. A dark end wall, in a long narrow room, will seem to advance—thus making the room appear more square, and less like a bowling alley.

<u>Cool colors</u> are blue, blue-green, blue-gray, violet. Basically "retreating colors," they make small rooms appear larger, give off a cooling, relaxing atmosphere, and are recommended for rooms with a southern exposure. Cool colors also have a mild sedative effect upon nervous, high-strung people.

To make any paint color but green look "warmer," add a little red to it. To warm green, add a little yellow. Conversely, to cool pink, green or gray, add a little blue. A very little green, plus a touch of blue, will cool ivory, yellow, cream or tan. When adding actual paint, use the same type as the main color. Add alkyd to alkyd; oil to oil; latex to latex. In using a colorant, be sure it's compatible with the paint. The label will tell you what type colorants should be used with the particular product you have chosen.

Room colors should harmonize for a pleasant effect, and a number of different basic schemes that can be used. Perhaps the most simple, and yet, in many ways, sophisticated method, is the monochromatic scheme. This utilizes a single color; the pure color, its tints, shades and tones. The analogous scheme embraces two primaries and all the colors between them, used in varied degrees of tints, shades and tones.

When planning color schemes, don't forget the woodwork, as its color must be incorporated into the decorating scheme. Draperies, lamp shades, vases, books, pictures and other furnishings, must also be included in the overall color scheme.

Complementary colors should not be used full strength on adjacent areas because each intensifies the other. If you want to use both red and green paint in the same room, for example, one of the colors should be grayed by adding some of its complement. Add some green to the red. Another way to moderate intensity is to tint one of the colors by adding white, or, darken it by adding black, thus producing a shade.

In applying the actual paint, care must be taken to prevent overlapping different colors, which will bring about a glazing condition that won't harmonize with the surrounding areas. The chart below clearly shows the drastic color changes that occur by overlapping.

GLAZING COLORS

If red overlaps green,	the result will be	brown
If red overlaps blue,	the result will be	violet
If blue overlaps green,	the result will be	greenish-blue
If red overlaps yellow,	the result will be	orange
If blue overlaps yellow,	the result will be	green
If green overlaps violet,	the result will be	slate
If violet overlaps orange,	the result will be	russet
If green overlaps orange,	the result will be	citron

Another point to remember: the larger the area, the darker the color. Keep this law of physics in mind when you choose a paint from a color card. The color on the inch-square chip will look much darker on the wall than on the chip. With this in mind, choose a slightly brighter color than you actually want, since it will darken when applied to a large surface. Also, remember that wet paint samples have a different appearance than dry paint will present.

And, as a final suggestion on color selection, shop with a definite color scheme, a positive, pre-determined pattern, in mind. You will then spend less money, and be more satisfied with the end result, than if you make numerous last minute changes and selections.

A Guide to Decorating Your New Home

INTERIOR

A decision as to which colors to use in remodeling or redecorating, can be easily reached—simply by your looking about and recognizing the answers when they are found. There is no need to engage an expensive decorator, since many solutions to the color problem are at your disposal.

For instance, a favorite painting may offer an excellent guide for a new color scheme, for, since it is your favorite painting, you must like its color scheme and the mood it creates. Acceptable color combinations and mood are the basic requirements for decorating, so take advantage of the professional color selection used by the artist, and decorate your home accordingly. The subject matter of the picture is unimportant; just concentrate on the proportions and blending of colors the artist has employed. The predominant color, which will represent about 65 per cent of the area, should be the background for your new scheme, to be used on walls and floors. The next prevailing color, which comprises about 25 per cent of an interior pattern, will probably be brighter, and perhaps will blend in with your furniture. The remaining 10 per cent will be sharper colors to bring out, or accent, the main colors.

A visit to the home furnishing departments of large stores, or to model homes open to public inspection, will provide professional interior decorating suggestions. Art galleries, designed in perfect color combinations, also might provide perfect answers for you, or, your present floor covering may be used as a guide, complementing the remaining hues from that basic color. Floor covering colors fall into four general groups, red, blue, brown and green, and the most commonly used colors in draperies and upholstery also come within these groups. With the floor covering used as the primary, the secondary colors for your walls can be easily selected. The chart below shows some suggestions for wall color that will be compatible with the indicated carpeting.

It is a good general rule to keep ceilings light, as deep colors are not for low rooms. In making this selection, keep in mind that the very lightest color appears darker on ceilings than on walls. Dark colors, which make ceilings appear lower

SELECTING FLOOR SHADES FROM CARPET COLORING

Carpet Color	Suggested Wall Color
brown tone	bone white, foam green, light ivory, peach bloom, cream, antique green, canary yellow, gray.
green tone	peach bloom, antique green, cream, canary yellow, foam green, bone white, gray.
blue tone	dusty rose, Wedgewood blue, canary yellow, light ivory, peach bloom, bone white, gray.
red tone	peacock blue, gray, robins egg blue, antique green, light ivory, foam green, light Wedgewood blue.

than they are, do not have the light reflecting qualities lighter colors afford.

Dark colors can sometimes be used to advantage on the end walls of a narrow room, making it appear more square. Colors that seem to make walls recede include: green, blue-green, turquoise, and blue. Colors having the opposite effect include: ivory, buff, peach, beige, dusty rose, and the so-called warm colors.

Remember, dark walls absorb light. However, well lighted rooms that do not have too much wall area, may be beautifully decorated by the use of dark colors, which eliminate glare. The effects of lights must also be considered, since fluorescent lights give off a blue color and increase the depth of other colors, while incandescent bulbs emit a red hue, and affect wall colors.

North and east side rooms, which receive a minimum of warmth from natural sunlight, should be decorated in warm colors. These include: dusty rose, copper, rose beige, coral, yellow, gold, or other members of the red-yellow family. Since

A Guide to Decorating Your New Home

north light is not direct sunlight, it reacts much the same as does fluorescent light, increasing depth of color, and having a tendency to inject a slight blue cast.

South and west side rooms receive full benefit of natural sunlight, so they should be decorated in cool colors. Light, airy tones, that take advantage of sunlight include: green, light blue, green-yellow, silver, light olive and other members of the green-blue family. When a neutral color is desired with bright furnishings, light grays and silver-grays can be used advantageously. The direct sunlight enjoyed by south and west rooms, contains orange and red, which will complement the cool colors.

LIVING ROOM

The living-room should be designed for relaxation, and yet have enough color animation to stimulate recreation and entertainment. If your family does little entertaining, a warm color will provide the necessary stimulation. Best advantages can be enjoyed by this type family through the use of a shade of any of the warm red-yellow colors, such as peach or rose.

When families are active and creative, or of the high-strung, nervous group, one of the sedative colors, of the green-blue family should be employed. If warm colors are used, they should be in delicate tints and tones that will provide a minimum stimulation effect. Flat paints, which diffuse light evenly, without glare, are recommended for walls and ceilings.

MASTER BEDROOM

Bedrooms should be decorated in cool, serene, sedative colors, for a soothing, restful atmosphere that will encourage relaxation and sleep. Various shades and tones of green, turquoise and blue, or any of the green-blue family, will give excellent results. For younger people, subdued shades of red may also prove satisfactory.

NURSERY

Contrary to popular belief, babies do not prefer baby blues and soft pink colors. They first recognize bright hues, and these colors have much appeal to them. For large walls, a deep peach will work well, while blue-green will give good results on narrow walls. In nurseries having natural furniture, the floor covering should be peach, gray or blue-green. There should also be some brilliant red accent, such as a lamp shade, toy box or other accessory.

TEEN BEDROOMS

A growing child spends many hours in his room, since it is the one place the child considers his very own. This room should be a place to study, relax, and "grow up" in, and the child should be allowed to select the colors most suited to his individual personalities and moods.

KITCHEN

Kitchens, the center of activity in a home, should be decorated in animated, lively, inspiring colors. Bright peach, yellow-orange or other colors of the red-yellow family create the proper atmosphere here. Some red should appear in the kitchen —in the floor covering, dishes, breakfast furniture, etc., to complement the red base colors. Pure yellow is not recommended, since it is a deep warm color, and often creates the impression that kitchens are too hot, even with air conditioning.

BATH

Bathrooms should be decorated in colors from the red-yellow family. They have the desired stimulating effect, and reflect a flattering light. Green and yellow-green enamels should be avoided whenever possible, in bathroom decorations.

A Guide to Decorating Your New Home

Gloss and semi-gloss paints and enamels, which provide the best moisture resistance, should be used in both kitchen and bathroom.

EXTERIOR

As with interior painting, there is no need to hire an expensive consultant's services for selection of exterior colors. The entire countryside is available for your observation—with each house offering new ideas and different patterns. Armed with notebook and pencil, take a Sunday drive through several modern residential areas, use, as a guide, houses constructed similarly to your own, as well as those with similar surroundings. In this manner, you can determine how your house will look, before the first brush of paint is ever applied.

Another good method of pre-determining exterior color schemes is to invest a few dollars in black and white photographs of your house. When you have narrowed down the color field, use water colors or wax crayons to apply the selected colors in given areas on the photos. This provides a first rate prevue of how the house will look when it's finished. This system also allows for changes in the planning stages, rather than after the work is in progress—when changes will be expensive.

In addition to your personal choice of colors, there are several other factors which enter into the selection of exterior paints. Foremost consideration must be given as to how your chosen colors will blend with the neighboring houses; and this is especially important when houses are set close together since nearby colors that clash harshly will detract from all the properties. Also consider surrounding trees, shrubbery, lakes, and other natural colors.

Generally speaking, exterior painting involves four distinct color areas: roof, siding, trim and accent. The accent area includes doors, shutters, screens, fence panels, etc., which are usually painted in contrast to the general house tone.

Light colors make a small house look larger; dark colors make a large house seem smaller. When light colors are used on an overly large house, a dark trim will help reduce the apparent structure size. Sharp trim colors on tall houses should be avoided, however, since the use of a dark color on the upper body, and a lighter color on the lower section, will make tall buildings look much lower. Shutters applied to upper story windows help create the same effect.

The roof is the key to the entire color scheme of a house. In building a new home, you'll have a wide range of selection, since roofing material color can be fairly well controlled. On existing homes, where the roof is still in good condition, the present color often imposes limitations.

White, pale gray, ice green, or other light color will make a small house appear larger. Darker colors should be used on two and three story buildings, to decrease their appearance. The average roof is designed to give 20 years service, so make your roof color selection carefully.

Many times extreme climates will enter into the roof color selection. A white roof reflects heat; a dark one absorbs heat. This can be proved by placing a piece of black cloth and a piece of white cloth on snow, in direct sunlight. Snow under the black cloth will melt rapidly; while snow under the white cloth will be relatively unaffected. Use of these two roof colors, in accordance with specific climate conditions, can effect heavy savings in heat and air-conditioning bills.

SIDING

While light colored siding is recommended for smaller houses, there should not be a sharp contrast between the siding and roof. A small house, or a low ranch-style structure, having both roof and siding of dark colors, gives a receded, diminutive appearance.

On large type houses, a darker tone of siding with a light roof will give a pleasing appearance. If part of the house is stone or brick, the color tone for siding should be picked up from that material. Sharp contrasts between the color of stone or brick, and the siding, breaks up the flowing architectural lines of the house, resulting in an awkward appearance.

A Guide to Decorating Your New Home

SUGGESTED COMPATIBLE COLOR SELECTIONS FOR ROOF, WALL, TRIM, AND ACCENT

Roof Color	Wall	Trim	Accent
forest green	light ochre pearl dusty rose	white med. ochre gray	forest green gray russet
pearl gray	white powder blue canary yellow	mist green white gray	light brown blue-green black
desert brown	dark orange light blue med. ochre	off-white powder blue lt. ochre	olive dark ochre russet
med. gray-blue	sea green powder blue jersey	white white white	blue-green dark brown dusty rose
speckled light gray	dusty rose white med. ochre	russet light ochre misty blue	brown dark green olive
gray-black	misty green white dark ochre	pearl gray off-white	black red olive
dusty rose	dark gray sea green dark brown	powder blue white jersey	white light orange light blue
Wedgewood blue	pearl light blue white	gray white dusty rose	white med. gray-blue rust
slate blue	white misty green Jersey	light gray-green dark pearl light orange	dark umber gray-green rust

TRIM

Much versatility in selection can be enjoyed with trim work. It can be the same color as the siding, a lighter tone of the same color, or in complete contrast—all with pleasant effect. Generally a most satisfactory trim paint can be achieved by adding white to the siding paint for a lighter shade of the same basic color. Or, where a pure white is not indicated, a small portion of siding color can be added to white, to give just enough tint to blend into the siding color.

ACCENT

While the accent represents a small percentage of a surface area, this phase of exterior painting can cause either success or havoc with the entire exterior scheme. Accent colors, unsuited for eaves, door or window trim, soffits, fascia or corner boards, usually work well on doors, window boxes, picture window frames, shutters on one-story levels, siding panels on homes of contemporary design, fence panels, etc. In choosing the accent paint, take into consideration the predominant colors in neighboring houses, to avoid serious clashing.

SCREENS

Regardless of the color scheme chosen, one problem always arises in exterior painting: what to do with screens.

Because we so often see screens and frames painted black, it seems more or less a tradition. Yet this is not a rule that must be followed, and there are several good reasons why other courses may be preferable. From a distance, dark colored screens on a light structure give a house the appearance of having black eyes, or ugly openings.

Thus, a good rule to follow is to paint screen frames the same color as the building frames into which they fit. Wire screening can also be painted the same color as the frames, but the screen enamel must be thinned down considerably to prevent clogging the mesh. Not only does this add to the house's appearance, but light-colored screens, which are much more difficult to see through from outside in the daytime, provide more privacy.

GABLES AND DORMERS

Gable ends, painted the same color as the siding, give small homes a larger appearance. On larger homes, or where architectural effects are to be emphasized, or where a vertical appearance is to be reduced, gable ends may be painted in trim colors. Combinations of colors, or stripes, are not recommended for this phase of exterior painting. Unattractive dormers can often be minimized by painting them the same color as the roof.

Very few people will be in complete color scheme agreement on any given house, but don't let criticism bother you—it comes to professional decorators all the time. As long as clashing colors have been avoided, and architectural lines have not been disrupted, don't worry about comments from sidewalk superintendents. It's *your* home, so, if the colors are agreeable to you and your family, consider your selection successful.